She Laughs

AMANDA BROWN COLEMAN

WESTBOW
PRESS®
A DIVISION OF THOMAS NELSON
& ZONDERVAN

WestBow Press books may be ordered through booksellers or by contacting:

This book is a work of non-fiction. Unless otherwise noted, the author and the publisher make no explicit guarantees as to the accuracy of the information contained in this book and in some cases, names of people and places have been altered to protect their privacy.

Scripture quotations are taken from THE HOLY BIBLE, NEW INTERNATIONAL VERSION®, NIV® Copyright © 1973, 1978, 1984, 2011 by Biblica, Inc.® Used by permission. All rights reserved worldwide.

WestBow Press
A Division of Thomas Nelson & Zondervan
1663 Liberty Drive
Bloomington, IN 47403
www.westbowpress.com
1 (866) 928-1240

Because of the dynamic nature of the Internet, any web addresses or links contained in this book may have changed since publication and may no longer be valid. The views expressed in this work are solely those of the author and do not necessarily reflect the views of the publisher, and the publisher hereby disclaims any responsibility for them.

Any people depicted in stock imagery provided by Getty Images are models, and such images are being used for illustrative purposes only. Certain stock imagery © Getty Images.

ISBN: 978-1-9736-3482-9 (sc)
ISBN: 978-1-9736-3481-2 (hc)
ISBN: 978-1-9736-3483-6 (e)

Library of Congress Control Number: 2018908568

Print information available on the last page.

WestBow Press rev. date: 8/9/2018

CONTENTS

DEDICATION

To our Savior, for His love, grace, and mercy.

To my wonderful husband Justin, who inspires me daily, and makes tag-teaming our chaos look easy.

To my children, Baker and Anna Benton, who have given me a love greater than I've ever known, and without whom, this book wouldn't exist.

To my Mama, an inspiration who persevered through many trials of her own.

To my Daddy, my heavenly angel hero.

To my Gran, from whom I inherited my spunk and sass.

To my Papa, our patriarch who embodies generosity. By example, he has taught us all to help those in need, and be an advocate for ourselves and others.

EPIGRAPH

66 She is clothed with strength and dignity and laughs without fear of the future" Proverbs 31:25

1

CHAPTER

With Trials Come Perseverance

Consider it pure joy, my brothers and sisters, whenever you face
trials of many kinds, because you know that the testing of your
faith produces perseverance. Let perseverance finish its work so
that you may be mature and complete, not lacking anything.
—James 1:2–4

I was born and raised in the Mississippi Delta. My weekdays
involved school and dance practice. Most of my weekends were
spent at my grandparents' house. I was raised in a Southern Baptist
family, you best believe my Sundays were spent in God's house. My
mom's parents, Gran and Papa, were at church every time the doors
were open and wherever they were, there I was also. My mom sang
in the choir, my brother played the piano, and I taught the preschool
Sunday school class. On the outside, I'm sure everything looked like
sunshine and rainbows, but home life was a different story.

I have many fond memories of my childhood, but there are certain parts that I would like to forget. While I've tried to bury deep some of the events that occurred, they are very much a part of me and the reason I am me.

At the age of two, my parents divorced, and afterward my brother and I lived with my mom, near my grandparents. Some of my fondest memories of my childhood are because of growing up around so much of my family. My three cousins lived nearby, and our crew of five was inseparable. Our summers were spent swimming at the pool, jumping on the trampoline, and riding four-wheelers through the country. We were more like siblings than cousins and we have remained close over the years.

At the age of eight, I lost my dad. He was a deputy at the sheriff's department and was killed in the line of duty during a domestic call, three days after my birthday. I will never forget my second-grade teacher tearfully leading me outside of the classroom, where Gran and Mama were standing there sobbing, waiting for me and my brother. Mama was crying so hard that I could barely understand her as she broke the news to us that Daddy was gone.

I remember riding home from school that day and replaying everything that had happened with Daddy the days before. He had given me a beautiful cross necklace and a pair of shoes for my birthday. We had just spent the weekend together at the carnival and I remember him trying to convince Mama to let me have a bunny (a real one) from a ring toss game.

One of the last weekends we spent together, I remember riding in his deputy car and asking him, "What if something bad happens?"

I'll never forget him saying, "Aww, Scoot, nothing bad is ever going to happen to me." He may have alleviated my fears at the time but it's almost ironic how he was taken from me, not long after saying that.

At such a young age, it was hard for me to grasp the permanent concept of death. It all seemed surreal. How could he be gone?

I don't remember crying that day or in the days following. I was more in shock than anything. It wasn't until hearing the twenty-one-gun salute at his funeral that I fell apart. He was honored as a hero, a Marine Corps Vietnam War veteran, and a law enforcement officer. But it broke my heart hearing the blasts of the very thing that killed him. I will never forget sobbing in my mom's arms while my aunt held my hand. It's amazing how much you can forget things over the years, but those memories will probably last me a lifetime.

Losing my daddy at such a young age forced me to grow up a little faster than my peers. My brother and I faced a harsh reality that many don't experience until much later in life. A year later, we lost my dad's mom, and I found myself sobbing at yet another funeral. Growing up without them makes me cherish the memories we had together so much more.

By the time I was nine years old, my mom remarried, and we moved away from my grandparents; we stayed in the same small city, but we were away, nonetheless. Our new home and life were getting off to a decent start but something was missing. My brother and I were still dealing with the loss of our daddy and grandmother, and our blended family wasn't meshing as well as we had hoped. Unfortunately, personality conflicts became a frequent issue. Despite efforts to remedy short fuses and attempts to compromise, there always seemed to be tension in the air. At times, that tension became volatile and our mother was stuck playing referee.

Growing up in an environment like that, I grew defensive and carried a chip on my shoulder, almost daring it to be knocked off. I was strong willed and determined to be the opposite of what I was exposed to. It sparked a flame inside of me and drove me to want more for myself.

In an effort to be away from "home" as much as possible, I spent the majority of my down-time at my grandparents' house and church. Romans 5:3–4 says, "And not only this, but we also exult in our tribulations, knowing that tribulation brings about perseverance." It was hard for me to understand the idea of rejoicing during what felt like agony, but I was desperate for God to intervene.

While I've always been quite passionate, I think growing up a in a home like that made me tough as nails; I had to be to stay sane. It gave me a backbone. It also gave me an interesting sense of humor and the determination to find the positives in a situation.

One huge positive for me is that I was blessed to have met my husband, Justin, at a young age. I know this will sound country, but one of my cousins introduced us. Justin and I started dating in high school. He was a senior and I was a junior at the time. This sweet, humble, quiet, solid rock of a guy was a godsend.

We are completely opposite in so many ways but it works for us. He's so reserved and I'm the Chatty Cathy carrying on full conversations with strangers at the grocery store.

I loved spending time with him and his family. They were an escape from my home. I could talk to him about anything and he was my shoulder to cry on. He became my rock and my best friend. I know God sent protection over me by placing Justin in my life when he did.

Everything was bliss until Justin left for college. Because he is a year older, he went away for school while I had to stay home to finish high school. Speaking of home, life had hit a new low. Things were worse than ever. Tempers were at an all times high and you could have cut the tension in the air with a knife. Every day seemed like a test. My brother left for college the year before Justin so there I was, alone, in what felt like a nightmare. That was one of the hardest years of my life—or so I thought. Stay tuned.

That's when I really started to read my Bible. I would shut my bedroom door and dig deep in God's Word. I started memorizing verses and would pray for God to change my situation. I wanted to be delivered from that evil, right then and there!

Once I left for college, life got better. I surrounded myself with friends, focused on completing my pre-requisites for nursing school, and stayed busy studying. Justin and I *survived* the long-distance college years (him at MS State and me at Ole Miss—Hotty Toddy!). I say *survived* because long-distance relationships take work. It wasn't always a cakewalk, but having him made life a lot easier, especially during those pivotal college years.

We got married while I was in nursing school and everything was falling into place beautifully. Justin got a great job at one of the insurance companies in the area. I graduated from nursing school and got my dream job in the emergency room at the children's hospital. My mom made some big changes and finally seemed be at peace. Life *was* grand.

Now, I don't want you to feel a sense of gloom and doom. That's not what this book is about. My childhood wasn't awful. We had good times, went on great vacations, and made lasting holiday traditions and memories. My mom is still my biggest fan and I couldn't do life without my Gran and Papa. *Everyone* needs to meet them—everyone! They are characters, and the "grand-apple" doesn't fall far from the tree.

I've shared all of this to say that the trials of my childhood made me strong. I wouldn't be the person I am today had I not been through them. As much as I don't like to talk about it, what I went through needed to be shared in order to gain a better understanding of who I am and the journey God chose for me.

I'm a firm believer in the saying "everything happens for a reason." and I truly believe those trials were God's way of preparing me for what was ahead. I didn't understand that at the time, but now, I can look back on that period and see tremendous spiritual growth as well as preparation for my future.

Take pains with these things; be absorbed in them,
so that your progress will be evident to all
--1 Timothy 4:15

Blindsided

Many are the plans in a person's heart, but it
is the Lord's purpose that prevails.
—Proverbs 19:21

We can make our plans, but the Lord determines our steps.
—Proverbs 16:9

I thought the entire experience of having children was going to be absolutely magical, every part of it. I just knew I would get pregnant immediately, only gain weight in my belly, and leave the hospital in prepregnancy clothes. That was cute...

Not only did I gain weight in my belly, I gained weight in every square inch of my body! It took us eleven months of trying to get pregnant with Baker. I had polyhydramnios (too much amniotic fluid—basically, Baker was swimming in an ocean) and gained seventy-eight pounds. That's right. I said SEVENTY-EIGHT pounds. I felt huge and I was miserable.

The magic wore off within the first few weeks when I was vomiting almost hourly. Carbs were life and I lived on Sprite and cheese toast during the first trimester. I distinctly remember thinking some not-so-sweet thoughts about my husband when I was sick as a dog and in need of a Sprite, to discover an empty box when I opened the refrigerator. I couldn't believe that he drank the last one. I may strive to be a Proverbs 31 wife, but in that moment, I saw RED. I was offended to my very core that he could be so inconsiderate and I held nothing back as I told him about it. And let me just tell you, that was the fastest I've ever seen him make a trip to Kroger and back!

Bless his sweet heart for having patience with me during that meltdown and the many meltdowns that followed. My family often joked that he was earning jewels in his heavenly crown for tolerating me. Gran often said, "poor Justin..." after I told her stories of my hormone-driven antics and to this day, we still occasionally hear a "poor Justin..." from her. I'm telling you, she's a character.

Baker came into this world as a toddler, weighing nine pounds and fourteen ounces. He skipped the newborn clothes stage and went straight to wearing three-month sleepers. He was absolutely adorable and I could have squeezed his scrumptious face off.

I was told big babies slept well so I had a false sense of hope going into our first night. When I say that child screamed his head off all night— Lord, have mercy! That baby was hoarse the next morning because he had made his presence known *all night*. The nurse in me knew his airway was clear because there's no way any fluid was left in his lungs after a night of constant screaming. Justin and I looked at each other at one point with a "Goodness! What have we done?" kind of look.

It turns out, our adorable little blonde-haired, blue eyed baby boy had colic. He screamed every single night from 9:00 p.m. until 2:00 a.m. for nine straight months. That was one of the most physically and mentally exhausting challenges I've ever faced. All I wanted was sleep. I spent the day caring for him, washing bottles, and washing clothes soiled with spit-up. I napped during the day to prepare for the bewitching hours that were awaiting me at night. At one point, in a sleep deprived stupor, Justin said, "I think we are being punished by

God." It wasn't a shining moment for parenthood but what can I say? It was rough.

We tried every colic trick in the book and took advice from everyone in an effort to console Baker's tummy aches. Sometimes, the only things that would keep him from screaming were running the vacuum, vent-a-hood, and kitchen sink, all in tandem. As you can imagine, our water and electricity bills were astronomical. At one point, I came close to inviting a priest with some holy water to cleanse my house from the evil that was upon us. I was almost convinced that he was possessed.

Our godsend of a pediatrician prescribed a reflux medication for Baker and he prayed for us at every office visit. We were battling Baker's colic and frequent ear infections so I kept his doctor on speed dial. To this day, I attribute any sanity I have left to his doctor. I don't know too many pediatricians who provide their personal cellphone numbers and answer an interrogation worth of questions at all times of the day. I'm telling you, he is a saint with the patience of Job! We are certainly beyond grateful for him.

Eventually, Baker learned to sleep and after his first set of ear tubes, we were finally able to enjoy our baby boy. It only took nine months! We were sleeping, he was happy, and once again, life *was* grand. Motherhood began to feel like what I always imagined it would be.

Baker gave us a few surprises and several trips to the emergency room because of croup and his need for oxygen and special breathing treatments. Despite that, we felt like we were rocking this whole parenthood thing. We were complete helicopters, and still are, but what can I say? Being a nurse in a pediatric emergency room will do that to you. He might as well forget about riding a skateboard or shooting a BB gun. If he even mentions it one day, I may throw him into a bubble!

After things got easy and we forgot about how awful colic was, we were ready for another baby. It couldn't happen to us twice, right?

My second pregnancy went much more smoothly, even with having to chase a toddler around. Justin and I found out we were having a girl and we were on cloud nine. But during the gender scan at seventeen weeks, the sonographer found choroid plexus cysts in her brain. Justin and I were very concerned but my doctor assured us that there was nothing to worry about yet, because most cysts resolve on their own. By the next ultrasound eight weeks later, the cysts had in fact, completely resolved. Despite that little scare, this pregnancy was much easier than my first. I was not as nauseated, I didn't have polyhydramnios, and I didn't gain seventy-eight pounds. Praise Jesus! Everything was perfect. Or so we thought...

The morning Anna Benton was born, was much like the morning Baker was born. Because of his size, *and* my size, I had to have a caesarean section. It was scheduled and it went smoothly with him. I assumed Anna Benton's delivery would be the same. I was much calmer the second time around and just eager to meet my girl. I couldn't wait to hold her.

After my doctor delivered her, she was handed to the neonatal nurse, and was taken to the infant warmer. Justin walked over there with them and was taking pictures. I heard the nurse tell him something but I couldn't understand what she said. I asked, "Is something wrong?" He came back over to me and said, "the nurse said her fingers are webbed. They need to check her out more." I was skeptical of what that meant, at the time, and was completely oblivious. And to be honest, I felt a little foggy because of the medications I was given. Fingers webbed? What did they mean?

I was rolled to recovery shortly after and more than ever, I was ready to see my girl. I mean, the first thing everyone does after having a baby is count ten fingers and toes, right? What did they mean by webbed fingers? What was taking them so long to bring her to me?

Justin stayed with Anna Benton in the nursery and I was nearly having a panic attack in the recovery room. I berated my nurse with questions and within minutes, the neonatologist walked in. Because of being a pediatric nurse, I knew I was headed for bad news. Neonatologists don't typically see parents until after the mother and baby are roomed. Sometimes, they don't make rounds with the mothers until the day after the baby is born. But there he was, right in front of me, looking concerned and solemn as a judge.

He said not only were Anna Benton's fingers fused together, her toes were too. Her anterior fontanelle (soft spot) extended from the bridge of her nose all of the way to the back of her scalp (3 to 4 times the size of what it should be). She also had a heart murmur. He said because she had so many congenital anomalies (birth defects), there was probably some type of genetic condition that had caused it all. He also said she needed to stay in the nursery a while longer to be closely monitored.

Since the day I found out I was having a girl, I dreamt of dance recitals, father-daughter dances, Barbie dolls, wedding planning, etc. While the doctor was speaking to me about genetics, cardiology, and plastic surgery referrals, I could see those dreams fading away. I was blindsided.

As I lay there completely numb from the waist down, all I wanted to do was get up and go see my baby. I needed to hold her. I needed to lay eyes on her. I needed to assess her myself. I needed to know that she was okay. Surely, she was ok! What could all of this be from? Why was it taking so long for them to bring her to me?

I've been scared before, but not like this. The sheer terror I felt was absolutely suffocating. I was beyond ready to be with her. My legs may have been completely numb but I was mentally preparing myself to crawl to the nursery if that's what it took to get to her. This Mama Bear was showing out and God bless my sweet nurse; she was so patient and attentive to me while I was laying there having a royal meltdown.

They *finally* brought her to me, swaddled and wearing her sweet pink cap with a bow. In that instant, everything stopped. The rest of the world didn't exist. Despite all of the scary information I had just heard, she was perfect. She was beautiful. She was my Anna Benton—my baby girl.

I stared into her big blue eyes and she stared back at me. I didn't think I could ever let her go. She was in my arms and she was safe.

The magnitude of that moment was breathtaking and will stay with me for the rest of my life.

From that day forward, Justin and I were changed. And by changed, I don't mean in just a parent with a new baby way. This felt different. We became her voice and her advocates.

After a few days in the hospital, we were discharged home. We were terrified of her and for her. We watched her like a hawk and were afraid for Baker to come near her. Because of her large anterior fontanelle, her head was basically all one soft spot and I couldn't take the chance of him accidentally bumping into her. Everything about her seemed so foreign to what we experienced with Baker as an infant. She may not have had colic but fear and that pain of worry in my gut never completely went away.

After about a week of settling into our new routine, we were thrown a curveball. After feeding and burping Anna Benton, her arms jerked, her eyes blinked, her head twitched, and her body fell limp. It may have looked like a textbook seizure but I was convinced that I was just paranoid because of all of the recent news we had been given. I refused to believe my child was seizing.

To be safe, I sent a message to the pediatric epileptologist at the children's hospital. He recommended an outpatient electroencephalogram (EEG— a test which detects seizures) and told me to keep him posted. A few minutes later, she began jerking again. This looked exactly like the episode she had before. That time, I knew she was seizing.

I tearfully screamed for Justin to scoop Baker up from the bathtub because we needed to take Anna Benton to the hospital. At that point, it had only been one week since having a C-section, so I couldn't drive. Justin got us to the emergency room in lightning speed and because I called my coworkers to let them know the situation, they were ready and waiting on us. Anna Benton continued to have seizures after we got there so they had to start an IV and give her medicines to stop them. I had done this a thousand times for my ER patients but it felt completely different when it was my own child who needed help. It was terrifying!

The first seizure medicine Anna Benton was placed on wasn't enough to stop her seizures. She needed an additional medicine in order for her seizures to be well controlled. Unfortunately, both of these medicines have side effects and require close monitoring. That basically means frequent lab draws to ensure appropriate medication levels in her blood.

We spent the next five days in the hospital as they ran a gamut of tests on her. I was post-partum, hormonal, and my world was crashing down on me. I found myself asking God, "Why?" What was supposed to have been one of the happiest times of my life, was becoming a nightmare. Watching Justin cradle our baby girl and sob over her nearly broke me in two. I dropped to my knees and begged God for help and mercy. We could have covered that hospital room floor with our tears. We were devastated.

Shortly after pouring my heart out, the lyrics to Casting Crowns "Praise You in This Storm" came to mind: "Every tear I've cried, You hold in Your hand. You never left my side and though my heart is torn, I will praise You in this storm."

I was absolutely broken but eventually, a sense of peace came over me. It took a little time but I was able to get to a place where I could start focusing on the positives in our situation: I am a pediatric nurse and we were in the hospital where I work. I knew everyone caring for her and knew she was in good hands. Because I had cared for patients with seizures many times, I was able to anticipate the protocol of tests that were performed on Anna Benton. Also, the wonderful epileptologist who I had spoken to earlier, happened to be the one on service that week. The stars were aligning for her and I know that was all because of God. I felt His presence with us, and He was seeing us through this.

The next few weeks and months were a blur, filled with appointments, genetic testing, and medication administration. We were feeling pretty weary at times and honestly, we felt scared to death. I watched her so closely, almost to the point of insanity. I had missed a seizure in the past. Really, I ignored it. But I couldn't forgive myself because of it and I was petrified of letting that happen again.

My wheels were constantly spinning and my mind never turned off. There was little, if any piece of mind felt. We needed a diagnosis with a prognosis, the final piece of the puzzle to help explain why all of this was happening. Our faith was tested multiple times. We were in the trenches and I found myself repeatedly asking God, "Why?"

I remember Justin asking me late one night as I was watching her sleep, "Haven't you been through enough? First everything that happened to you as a kid, then Baker having colic, and now this? Why can't we catch a break?"

I'm going to be honest. Justin saying that made me go through some of the rough times of my childhood. It brought up the sting of losing my Daddy so young. It made me miss him even more, knowing that he didn't get to see me grow up, or meet Justin and our kids. From there, I let my mind wander to some of the harsh memories of growing up in a broken, blended home. It has taken a lifetime for some of those scars to heal. Then, I started thinking of the patients I have cared for whose mothers were admittedly negligent while pregnant, yet had completely healthy babies. I wasn't exactly the picture of health while pregnant; I never worked out and I could suck a donut or three down like a boss. But for the most part, I did everything "right" yet my baby wasn't completely healthy. She was fragile. It didn't seem fair that we had been through so much and I was becoming bitter. And *boy* do I mean bitter. Life was not turning out how I had planned and I was pouting about it.

When it was time for me to go back to work, we put Anna Benton in our church daycare. It was the same place Baker attended. I was a nervous wreck not being with her but at the time, I felt I didn't have another option. I gave the staff a list of phone numbers as well as information about seizure precautions. I kept my cell phone in my scrubs pocket and was ready to answer it at all times.

During Anna Benton's third day at daycare, the director called. She said they could only get Anna Benton to wake up for a few minutes at a time. They didn't see any seizure activity but were concerned something was wrong. I left the hospital in a hurry, so rushed that I'm not even sure I clocked out. I sped to the daycare and was back in the ER with her within a matter of minutes. We had hoped she was just drowsy from her seizure medicines but her lab work proved otherwise. Her medication levels were low which means she probably had a breakthrough seizure. She required yet another EEG and an admission to the step-down unit.

It was during that hospitalization that Justin and I decided I needed to quit full-time work and stay at home. At first, I was conflicted. Being a nurse is so much a part of who I am. I love the pediatric ER and I was going to miss it, but I knew I needed to be the one caring for Anna Benton.

Let me tell you, being a stay-at-home-mom (SAHM) may sound glamorous, but it was hard work and every day brought a new challenge. Potty training a toddler while having an infant with special needs was a lot to handle. Much like his mother, Baker Coleman was blessed with an extra dose of stubborn, so I felt like I had climbed Mount Everest by the time he transitioned to underoos. And in hindsight, we probably should have had a ceremony or something of the sort, to mark such a momentous occasion. Lord, have mercy...

And then there was the time he locked me out of the house. I had walked a few feet out of the door to check the mail and came back to the dead-bolt locked. I could see through the side lights and there he was, grinning, proud as all get-out, with his sippy cup in hand. Anna Benton was in her bouncy seat and was mesmerized by cartoons. They were both completely fine but I panicked. As much as I tried to get Baker to unlock the door that he had so proudly locked, it wasn't happening. I ran to our neighbor's house, called Justin at work, and told him to fly home. In the meantime, I stood on the front porch and watched them, begging Baker to unlock the door. But, he wouldn't. In fact, he kept laughing.

It was until he drank every bit of his juice and needed more, that he realized he needed *me*. He kept demanding more juice in his cup and I kept demanding for him to unlock the door. This standoff lasted about fifteen minutes until finally, Justin drove up. He didn't say a word. He just smiled and handed me his keys. I unlocked the door, grabbed Baker up (to keep him from doing it again), and handed Justin his keys so he could go back to work. I may have been flustered but we were both fighting back laughter as he backed out of the driveway. We were both completely tickled but we couldn't let Baker know it.

To this day, we still bring up that story and you best believe I put that in his baby book. I may even bring it back up at his high-school graduation or wedding reception. That's the privilege of payback and parenting, right?

Having to carry two small children all over creation proved to be a task at times also. There were plenty of times we rolled up to appointments on two wheels. (I'm still tempted to slap a "Coleman kids taxi service" sign on the side of my car.) I learned to stay ready, so I didn't have to get ready.

Some days were absolutely amazing but there were also days Justin would come home from work to find me standing at the door, with car key in hand. This mama needed an attitude adjustment and five minutes of peace and quiet! To get some *me* time, retail therapy wasn't in the budget, so I drove around or just parked in an empty lot. Depending on what went down that day, I either rested in the quiet or had the radio blaring (usually on KLove) so loudly that I couldn't hear myself cry. I used that *me* time to decompress and pray. So much had changed in just a matter of months and I had no control over it. I felt helpless, vulnerable, and at times, afraid of our future. Everything we had planned was almost completely different than what was actually happening. Life had gotten real and hard, quickly. And I told God *all* about it.

Even though it was difficult at times, I am beyond grateful for having the opportunity to stay home. I wouldn't trade that time for the world and I hold dear, the memories made. Some of my favorite memories from that time are of Baker and I snuggling on the couch and watching cartoons while surrounded by his entourage of stuffed animals, playing dress up with Anna Benton and laughing all day, and nap time. I loved watching them sleep, so innocently and peacefully. I would stare in awe of my beautiful babies, counting my blessings, and thanking God for letting me be their Mama. Speaking of nap time, I occasionally caught a little shut-eye myself. Sleep when they sleep, right?

So yeah, we were thrown a couple of curveballs. Things had not turned out like we expected. We anticipated some change with bringing home a second child, but almost nothing was the same. Even though we felt broken and our world was completely different, we slowly began picking up the pieces, put them back together, and somewhere along the way, discovered our new normal. I still questioned God often but knew He was with us then, and for whatever was ahead.

> Have I not commanded you? Be strong and courageous.
> Do not be afraid; do not be discouraged, for the LORD
> your God will be with you wherever you go.
> —Joshua 1:9

3

Great Expectations

Immediately Jesus, aware in His spirit that they were
reasoning that way within themselves, said to them, 'Why
are you reasoning about these things in your hearts?'
—Mark 2:8

I am a creature of habit and I am set in my ways. I am also a
borderline control freak. Parenthood, in general, changed me and
taught me that I am really not in control of anything. I am no longer
in charge of just me. There is another life that I am responsible for
now; a life that requires frequent intervention: sheltering, feeding,
changing, clothing, et cetera.

Justin and I had been together for almost ten years by the time
Baker entered the picture. We were kids in high school when we
started dating and we had a lot of growing up to do—me, more so,
than him. Before kids, I was selfish and self-centered. Life involved
doing *what* I wanted, *when* I wanted. I was on no one else's schedule,
but my own. Consumed with my life, I was usually distracted from

what was going on around me. Unfortunately, to this day, that is still a problem, but I'm working on it. Thank you, Lord, for grace.

Vanity was an issue also. I wouldn't leave my house without perfect hair and make-up, even if it was just for a quick trip to the grocery store. There is nothing wrong with wanting to look nice but I can assure you, I was doing it for all of the wrong reasons.

I roll my eyes at that version of myself. How childish and immature. What was so important to me then, makes me laugh now.

Even though we felt we were mature enough to start a family, we still had a lot of growing up to do. I'm embarrassed to say that while pregnant with Baker, I specifically prayed for a blonde-haired, blue eyed boy. While I also prayed for him to be healthy, having a beautiful baby was so important to me. I was foolish, among other things, to make that prayer such a priority. Again, I roll my eyes.

Once Baker came along, we found ourselves up most of the night with a colicky infant. Clinging to every second of sleep I could get, my vanity and selfishness were quickly fading. Coffee and dry shampoo were life and you know what? There just wasn't enough time in the day for work outs, spray tans, and teeth whitening trays anymore. It was evident from the day he was born, we were on his schedule. We catered to his every whim, especially if it meant he wasn't crying in pain or frustration. Any plans I made during the day were quickly replaced with naps instead.

Because of having a child, our priorities were changing and decisions became more about our family of three instead of just ourselves. Outside obligations became much less important.

As Baker grew into the toddler stage, I realized even more, how little control I had. He was absolutely adorable but he was a tyrant. Yes, I am his mother. It is my job to raise him to not be a jerk, and you better believe I discipline him when he acts like one. But, he is strong-willed and he tests me. Oh, have mercy, that child tests me. (I learned not to pray for patience because you don't just wake up one day with a little extra. You get tested even more, in order to become more patient.)

Justin and I were brave and had our kids twenty-seven months apart, so Baker was freshly into the Terrible Twos when Anna Benton was born. Unfortunately for him, everything that was going on with her left our fuses a little short. Like with most toddlers, feeding him sometimes turned into a stand-off because what foods he loved the day before, he absolutely loathed the next. His meltdowns were truly something to behold and they usually ended with both of us in tears.

Counting to three didn't work for this tiny terror; there was no negotiating with him. He pitched several fits while we were in public, resulting in a "Come to Jesus meeting" in front of everyone. If I tried to excuse us to another room, it would end up being a bigger scene than if I just nipped it in the bud, right where we stood. Now, before this goes off on a tangent about how to discipline, I'm going to stop right there. This isn't that kind of book.

Baker may have given us a run for our money at that age, but I wouldn't trade him for the world. He turned from a cantankerous dictator into a sweet, kind-hearted, affectionate little boy. He may have put us through the ringer and humiliated us multiple times, but we can laugh about it now.

I can honestly say, that year was pretty rough. It was probably our hardest year to date, especially the winter. Anna Benton had been hospitalized almost monthly because as she would grow and gain weight, she would have breakthrough seizures. That resulted in an increase in her medications. Genetic testing continued but we were nowhere near a diagnosis.

That December, Baker was hospitalized for croup and hypoxia (oxygen requirement) for several days. Almost immediately after we brought him home, Anna Benton was hospitalized for a new type of spells. After a video EEG and the addition of another medicine to stop the new spells, she was discharged—two days before Christmas. Santa's sleigh was more like the struggle bus that year and not a single present was wrapped. Oddly enough, that became a tradition and we kind of love it that way.

But honestly, that winter hurt my feelings. I remember posting on social media during that time, about feeling like Job. As soon as we would start feeling comfortable, the rug would get pulled out from under us again, reminding me of the verse, "the Lord giveth, and the Lord taketh away" (Job 1:21).

Our family was going through so much and once again, I felt like my world was crashing down. I had no control. And per my usual, I was asking God, "Why?" "Why didn't we have a diagnosis yet?" "Why were we blindsided, especially so often?" During AB's pre-Christmas hospitalization, I was sitting in that hospital crib, holding my grinning baby girl, telling God, "If you are trying to get my attention, Lord, you've got it." But in reality, I was doing too much whining and not enough praising.

I wanted control and I wanted answers. Knowledge is power, right? Parenthood may have forced me to grow up but I was still *so* immature. My spray tans and daily hair washes may have fallen by the wayside, but everything was still focused on me and what I wanted. And at that point, *I* was the toddler throwing a fit.

This whole motherhood thing is a lot harder than I could have ever imagined. The young, vain, and selfish version of me pictured it to be more like playing house. The problem with that is that I never dreamt of anything going wrong; that things wouldn't turn out like I expected, or that there would be times that tested my faith and brought me to my knees.

Being a parent is not always rainbows and sunshine. Being a mom is one of the hardest things I've ever done, but it is by far the most rewarding. It is breathtakingly beautiful, yet real and raw. And thank goodness, God has more patience with me and my toddler fits, than I had with Baker during his.

> Because of the Lord's great love, we are not
> consumed, for his compassions never fail. They are
> new every morning; great is your faithfulness.
> —Lamentations 3:22–23

4

CHAPTER

Too Much to Bear

Fear not, for I am with you; be not dismayed, for I am
your God. I will strengthen you, yes, I will help you. I
will uphold you with My righteous right hand.
—Isaiah 41:10

1 Corinthians 10:13 says, "No temptation has overtaken you that is not common to man. God is faithful, and he will not let you be tempted beyond your ability, but with the temptation He will also provide the way of escape, that you may be able to endure it." I struggle with the saying, "God will never give you more than you can handle." The way I interpret it is that He won't tempt you more than you can handle but He may give you load larger than you can bear alone. And for me, He did.

I was blindsided with what would be a lifetime of not living in the norm and caring for a child in a perpetual infant stage. I was overwhelmed and broken, trying to wrap my head around what I expected my life to be versus what it actually was. I believe He brought me to my knees and allowed me to be broken, to teach me to rely solely on Him. He used my struggles to teach me to trust Him.

I wanted Anna Benton to be normal. I wanted a diagnosis, something that would help explain why all of this was happening. There had to be a syndrome or some type of genetic connection among her seizures, polysyndactyly (fused fingers and toes), heart defects, and skull abnormalities. If we had a diagnosis, that might mean a possible treatment, prognosis, or at least allow us to gain insight into what we could expect for her future.

We were receiving a lot of negative results with genetic testing and the doctors were able to start ruling out what she didn't have. While negative results are a blessing, I felt completely in the dark. It seemed like we were spinning on a never-ending hamster wheel and no closer to an answer. All the while, with every test meant more discomfort for her. She was scanned, x-rayed, poked, and prodded, and it broke my heart watching her go through it all.

As time passed and we were waiting on more results, we noticed Anna Benton wasn't reaching milestones like other children her age. She started rolling over on time, but she had head lag as well as low muscle tone in her abdomen. She wasn't fixing on and following objects. She wasn't reaching for them either. She was so happy and completely content just lying there, with no stimulation from anyone or anything. While we are grateful for such a happy baby, we knew something wasn't right and I began to fear the worst. Again, those dreams of dance recitals and playing dress up continued to fade away.

We spent a lot of time with her neurologist during the next appointment. We heard a lot of "we will just have to wait and see as she grows to know what to do next." It makes complete sense but patience is not my strong suit. I had spent almost her entire lifetime in a rush-to-wait type of mindset. One negative test result would lead to a rush to get the next test ordered, followed by waiting for that result. Even though we would try to keep our minds off of the tests and just take one day at a time, the waiting seemed endless. That particular appointment resulted in a physical therapy and ophthalmology referral.

We knew from birth that Anna Benton would need surgery to separate her fingers but at the time, thought it served more of a cosmetic purpose. There was more to it than that.

Part of the reason she didn't grasp objects was because her fingers were fused. They were connected in such a way that they resembled what was once called lobster hands. (Thank goodness, medical terminology has become a little more politically correct, but that is indeed how she used her hands.) As I watched her struggle to hold a rattle or really *anything*, I was more willing to accept the fact that she would need surgical intervention in order for her to develop fine motor skills.

She had two surgeries on her hands, one at four months old and one at ten months old. These micro surgeries were very intricate and involved the separation of vessels in her hands and fingers, in order to provide proper circulation to each newly separated digit. Skin grafts were taken from her groin to supply enough tissue to form each finger. With each surgery, she had casts above her elbow for a week, followed by daily dressing changes for several weeks.

In short, those weeks were difficult. Wrapping gauze around each one of her tiny fingers was tedious and she often cried through each dressing change.

But like always, Anna Benton was a trooper. I kid you not, that child was still trying to roll over with two heavy pink casts on her arms and five-inch incisions on her hips; all with a smile on her face. She is superwoman! Her dexterity improved with both surgeries and she started weekly occupational therapy to promote fine motor development.

A visit to her ophthalmologist resulted in a diagnosis of hyperopia (far sightedness) and glasses. She got her first pair at nine months old. They were pink and she looked absolutely adorable in them. Once her vision was corrected, she began watching us and became enthralled with Baker. She thought everything he did was wonderful (and still does).

Ironically, we had put so much faith in surgery and glasses, but they weren't the magic solutions for all of her delays. Surgery improved dexterity in her hands and better vision increased her awareness of her surroundings. But head lag, along with poor muscle tone in her trunk, were still major issues. Anna Benton was able to roll over but was showing no signs of being able to sit up.

We reinforced physical and occupational therapy almost constantly at home. I felt like every bit of progress was heading in the direction of something bigger. If she reached for an object, I would praise her, then push her to pass it from one hand to the other. I was so motivated for her to advance, it was like I was *willing* her to do it, as if I could speak it into existence. But that kind of perseverance can only be sustained for so long and I wasn't prepared for if or when her development plateaued.

Milestones were slow to come for Anna Benton and once she was around six months old, they became almost stagnant. I would get my hopes up, then have my heart broken when she wasn't able to do what I was pushing her to do.

I would pray for progress and would beg the Lord to allow her to catch up. I prayed the same prayer every single night: for both of my children to be happy, healthy, and developmentally appropriate. I had faith the Lord could completely heal Anna Benton (and still do) but I was terrified that it isn't part of His plan.

Matthew 7:7–8 says, "Ask and it will be given to you; seek and you will find; knock and the door will be opened to you. For everyone who ask receives; the one who seeks finds; and to the one who knocks, the door will be opened." I recalled Luke 16:10, "He who is faithful in what is least is faithful also in much" and also Luke 17:6, while having "faith of a mustard seed" that she could catch up with milestones. Anna Benton had an army praying for her and I just knew that those prayers of healing that were flooding the gates of heaven would be answered.

While all of that was going on with Anna Benton, we started noticed more profound sensory and processing issues with Baker. He had always been a little quirky, but we felt there was nothing beyond that. He stimmed (flapping his hands and tip-toe walking) with excitement and nervousness and simple things like brushing his hair or brushing his teeth were almost guaranteed to cause a meltdown. He struggled with activities requiring concentration and coordination like playing baseball, playing on playground equipment, and riding a bike. He required excessive repetition to master a skill and things (stimming and meltdowns) seemed to get worse if there was a variance in his routine. Before we knew it, he was referred for occupational therapy (OT) and my "Coleman kids taxi service" was utilized even more.

I'm still waiting on Justin to make me a magnet for the car.

I would hear praises from friends and family of all of the things their children could do. It would hurt my feelings even more because my babies couldn't do a lot of those things. It became exceptionally hard when children younger than Anna Benton were surpassing her, developmentally, and I will never forget sting I felt when a child younger than her called her a baby. Justin felt that sting too. It tugged at my heart a little bit when I saw a friend post a video on social media of her son knocking a baseball out of the park and one of him riding his bike. I wasn't jealous; I was just struggling to accept the fact that my kids aren't the poster children for normal. And all of these comparisons I was making weren't helping me, or them.

But with time a *lot* of OT, we have seen leaps and bounds in improvement with Baker. It took us four seasons of baseball to realize that it wasn't just because of sensory-processing issues that he was struggling; it's just not his thing. But, he can now ride a bike with training wheels and can climb the rock wall at the playground. He's proud. I'm proud. We're all proud.

Despite Baker's improvements, bitterness was settling into my heart faster than I could stop it. My prayers started changing from helpless and broken, to flat out mad. I was so angry that we were going through the trenches and because both of my kids were struggling (in different ways).

On top of that, I had the notion to go back to school to get my master's degree, in order to become a nurse practitioner. I signed up for the Graduate Record Exam (GRE), a test which is required for most graduate school programs and I made an appointment with the director of the pediatric nurse practitioner program. Our meeting went great and I was looking forward to starting back to school. I always said I would go back and instead of just taking one year off, I had taken four years. The very next day after I met with the director, Justin woke up with a temperature of 103. Shortly afterward, Anna Benton's fever spiked. Turns out, they both had the flu. And immediately, my wheels were spinning. How was I going to go back to school, study, go to class, go to clinical, etc. with a child who couldn't go to daycare? Our families are almost two hours away and I felt too guilty to ask them to keep her that much.

Justin and I are a tag team and we do well to get everything taken care of on a day-to-day basis. With me being back in school and if he got sick again, I knew there was no way we could manage everything.

We had a long talk and I realized going back to school just wasn't in the cards for me. I cancelled my reservation to take the GRE, lost my deposit, and took a day or two to finish pouting. Per my usual, I told God *all* about it. And then after praying so angrily, I would feel guilty for said anger.

There were times I felt abandoned by God while recalling verses like, "Come, all you who are weary and heavy laden, and I will give you rest" (Matthew 11:28) and that He will never leave us or forsake us (Hebrews 13:5). I know our circumstances could have been (and could be) much worse, but that didn't make it easier for me to accept them. I was so conflicted and I isolated myself from the world. I flip-flopped from being hurt and angry, followed by overwhelming gratitude that Baker is so high-functioning and that Anna Benton isn't as medically compromised as other children. I was an emotional roller coaster, not just on a daily basis, but an hourly one.

One Sunday morning during Lifegroup, our teacher covered anger and said something so profound that resonated with me. To this day, I still recall it when I find myself angry on a hard day. He said, "God can handle you being mad at Him. He's *pretty* tough. He can take it." He referenced Psalm 137, a prayer of bitterness and anger. It proves He can hear us at our worst and still love us unconditionally. While we aren't supposed to let our anger become sin (Ephesians

4:26–27), we aren't supposed to hide it from Him either. He can take it and He can heal it.

It was during that time that I learned to celebrate Anna Benton's small victories. Before then, I was so determined for her to develop on time and spent so much time being hurt about it, I had missed out on opportunities for joy.

Regardless of what she endured, she remained blissfully happy. She's pretty amazing (I will elaborate on that soon) and if I had focused more on *her* joy and less on *my* pain, I wouldn't have missed those beautiful moments.

Some of my favorites of Anna Benton's little victories are: when she grabbed her own foot for the first time (especially because she had been on a medicine for muscle spasticity for most of her life), when she ate a cheerio for the first time, and when she held an Oreo and put it to her mouth to eat it. Those victories may seem little to most but they are *huge* for us. We may still say little victory often, but we mean it in a *big* way.

A conversation with my mother-in-law helped bring a little perspective to my situation. I guess you can say Justin and I were a little disappointed that baseball wasn't Baker's thing. She brought to light that she and my father-in-law went through something similar with Justin. Justin's dad is the jack-of-all-trades type and can build pretty much anything with his bare hands. He's an engineer and has always been pretty handy. Justin, however, is not. Unfortunately, he and I both are pretty domestically challenged, which provides multiple opportunities for comedic relief as we troubleshoot home ownership.

I digress.

Justin knew early on in college that engineering wasn't his thing. At first, his dad was disappointed, as he had plans for Justin to take over his business eventually. But even with heavy pressure for engineering, Justin found his niche in insurance and financial risk management. Not only that, he excelled in it. He chose that as his career path and graduated with honors. While Justin may not have chosen the field that his dad expected, no one could be prouder of him. His career path allowed me to eventually be a SAHM, so I would say it worked out alright.

And that's exactly how we need to be with Baker and baseball. As much as I love to see that cutie pie in his baseball uniform, I will be completely okay if he never wants to play again. He has proven time and time again that baseball is not his thing. It may sting a little but honestly, I just want him to be happy with whatever he chooses to do. If building robots is more his thing and means I'm spending the weekends at competitions rather than the ball fields, I will still be his biggest fan.

I'm also grateful that Baker is so smart. He's pretty amazing. He may not be able to physically do some of the activities of his peers but he is able to progress scholastically with them. He's my little concrete thinker who is always inquisitive. He loves to learn. At two, he showed off his mad organizational skills by arranging all of his Mickey Mouse stuffed animals according to size, from smallest to largest. He loves counting and math problems. (My father-in-law still may get his engineer. He may just have to wait a generation later.) He's a whiz kid with his Nintendo and I have yet to beat him at Mario Kart. (I'm serious. It's not for a lack of effort. I try hard. He's just that good!) I also don't know any other five-year-old who drew a color-coded picture of their dad for Donuts with Dad at school, complete with a heart, lungs, kidneys, stomach, and trachea. That's right, a trachea, and it was blue!

I fully intend to bank my retirement on that kid. Totally kidding. Sort of..

I have faith that God can heal Anna Benton and alleviate Baker's sensory-processing issues. I also have faith that if it is not in His plan for her to be healed, for him to improve, or for me to go back to school, He has our best interest at heart. He will protect us and guide us through this journey (Jeremiah 29:11).

I may occasionally feel like my load is too heavy to bear but I need to talk to Him about it every step of the way, trusting that His plan is greater than my own. After all, He can see the bigger picture, while

I can't. Some of my prayers may be ugly but it is important that my trials don't overcome my faith.

For I am convinced that neither death nor life, neither angels nor demons, neither the present nor the future, nor any powers, neither height nor depth, nor anything else in all creation, will be able to separate us from the love of God that is in Christ Jesus our Lord.

—Romans 8:38–39

5
CHAPTER

Hard Lessons Learned

Do not be quick in your spirit to be angry, for irritation settles in the bosom of fools. Do not say, 'Why were the earlier days better than these days?' for it is not from wisdom that you inquire this.
—Ecclesiastes 7:9–10

We are to humble ourselves and cast our cares on Him; He will bear them, carry us, and deliver us (1 Peter 5:6–7 and Isaiah 46:4). I have never felt so helpless than when I have had to rush my sick, seizing child into the emergency room. While I may have cared for seizing children a thousand times prior, it is a totally different experience when it is my own child who needs care. It is terrifying.

I've also never felt humbler, handing her over to the nurse anesthetist to take her into the operating room. Or for the weeks following surgery, involving scheduled pain medicine, cast care, and frequent dressing changes. Other parents were planning play dates while we were arranging therapies and post-operative care. It didn't seem fair that my baby girl, so small and so innocent, had to go through so much. I felt helpless and as usual, I told God *all* about it.

Like I said before, bitterness was settling into my heart faster than I could stop it. I was so angry all of the time and I found myself once again, carrying a chip on my shoulder, daring someone to knock it off. Questions like, "Does she really need those glasses?" and remarks like, "It must be nice to stay at home" would nearly set me off. It took every bit of self-restraint I had not to go completely Mama Bear on those people. I know they meant no harm and had no clue they were pouring salt into a wound the size of Texas, but it hurt just the same.

Everything was becoming a trigger for anger, even little things. I will never forget one brave woman asking me, "Do you feed your baby chocolate?" as Anna Benton lay in car seat, four months old and two weeks post-op from her first hand surgery. I was completely puzzled at this lady's question but intrigued enough to say, "No, ma'am. Why do you ask?" She said, "Well it looks like chocolate! Something is all over her hands."

I was completely dumbfounded and honestly, I needed to pause because I was afraid of what I might say to that brazen woman. I explained that Anna Benton had just had surgery and the dark substance she was referring to on her hands was sutures. Praise God, I didn't say anything out of sorts. I'm sure the look on my face and the tone of my voice said enough though. I was so upset that she asked that and I vented to the world about it (a downside to social media). My feelings were hurt and I needed justification for my anger. Within minutes, I had a cheering section (more like angry mob) of folks that were ready to practically verbally assault a perfect stranger in mine and Anna Benton's honor.

Another opportunity for bitterness to creep into my heart is when someone comments about Baker stimming. A man once jokingly called him "twinkle toes" at the ballfield, as he stimmed from the batter's box to first base. Baker was so proud for hitting the ball and he couldn't help himself. Other kids would have run like lightning after a hit like that but bless him, he tip-toed the whole way. I was so proud that he gave 100 percent with that hit and I didn't care that he stimmed all of the way to first base.

And notice I said that he was only called "twinkle toes" *once*. While I didn't open my mouth, I must have given the man who said that, a look that sent chills down his spine. Baker definitely stimmed again but I can assure you, not another comment was made by that man. Mama Bear, for the win!

Ecclesiastes 7:9 says, "Do not hasten in your spirit to be angry, for anger rests in the bosom of fools." Luke 6:45 says, "A good man brings good things out of the good stored up in his heart, and an evil man brings evil things out of the evil stored up in his heart. For the mouth speaks what the heart is full of." My heart stayed full of hurt and bitterness and I displayed it for all of the world to see. Looking back at that chocolate-on-the-hands situation, all I can say is: Thank you, Lord, for grace, and mercy, and forgiveness!

Let me tell you, negativity consumed me! When I let my mind go there, I lived there, wallowing in self-pity. It seemed easier to be bitter than to face my fears and feelings. There were some days where I had to make a conscious effort to not be a jerk (especially after a sleepless night when Anna Benton had her days and nights mixed up). Other parents were complaining their child had too many after-school activities or their child talks too much. I was on the opposite end of the spectrum, wishing those were our only problems.

I broke down in tears when I applied for our first handicap tag for Anna Benton. There was something upsetting about having physical proof in hand that we were headed down a different and somewhat unknown path.

The same feelings welled up when she eventually needed surgery to have a gastrostomy tube (g-tube) placed when we couldn't get her to eat or drink enough to maintain an adequate weight. It is common for children with special needs to get a g-tube. They can't control a lot of what goes on in their world, but one thing they *can* control is what they eat. And that's exactly what Anna Benton did. She would clamp those lips, locked up tighter than Fort Knox. No food was getting through them. She would do this for several meals a day, several days a week. And because of that, getting her to maintain her weight was a losing battle. Our solution? A g-tube. (Medical advancements for the win!)

While we are grateful to have access to resources that can improve her quality of life, handicap tags, g-tubes, feeding pumps, home health supplies etc. scream, "SPECIAL NEEDS!" I was just *so* consumed with everything Anna Benton wasn't able to do, with bitterness, with finding a diagnosis, with our lack of "normal," etc., that I allowed myself to pout about it. Once again, I was missing out on opportunities for joy.

It was around that time that I heard Lauren Daigle's song, "I will trust in You." Have you ever heard something that resonated with you so profoundly? Literally every word spoke to my current situation. As Lauren said, God wasn't moving the mountains I needed Him to move and He wasn't parting the waters I wished I could walk through. But unlike her song, I was so bitter and consumed with *me*, I wasn't trusting Him.

Instead, I was praying, and whining, and throwing a toddler fit. I knew He was there. I could feel His presence with me but I wasn't trusting His plan for my life, and certainly not for Anna Benton's. It was time for a change. It was time for me to listen. And it was time for me to trust God.

He is not afraid of bad news; his heart is firm, trusting in the Lord.
—Psalm 112:7

The Lord bless you and keep you; the Lord make his face shine on you and be gracious to you; the Lord turn his face toward you and give you peace.
—Numbers 6:24–26

6

CHAPTER

Suffering

All the world is full of suffering. It is also full of overcoming.
—Helen Keller

The thief comes only to steal and kill and destroy. I came
that they may have life and have it abundantly.
—John 10:10

We are all sinners and if you're like me, it is hard to admit fault. I have told you plenty about my pride, selfishness, vanity, bitterness, etc. And those faults are barely scratching the surface. I fail God daily and I am so thankful for His mercy and grace.

Up to this point, I have painted a very "woe is me" picture but I promise, I'm getting to the point. I have told you so much about how differently my life has been from what I expected. You've heard my groanings of how challenging it has been, raising a child with special needs. As embarrassed as I am to admit that I felt that way for so long, I am grateful for the opportunity to share my story of God's goodness.

The Bible is full of passages regarding the punishment for sin: "For the wages of sin is death..." (Romans 6:23), "All have sinned and fallen short of the glory of God." (Romans 3:23), "All who sin apart from the law will also perish apart from the law, and all who sin under the law will be judged by the law." (Romans 2:12). To sin is to be apart from God and where there is sin, there is suffering. Because we have sinned, we deserve death but praise Him, He loved us enough to spare us from what we deserve. That's grace.

"For our sake He made Him to be sin who knew no sin, so that in Him, we might become the righteousness of God" (2 Corinthians 5:21). God sent his holy Son, Jesus Christ, to suffer a horrible death, as the ultimate sacrifice, to pay for our sins. He was beaten, bruised, stabbed, starved, and hung to a cross. He experienced one of the most horrific deaths imaginable in order to spare us from our sinful fate, so that we may spend eternity with Him. He paid it all, all because He loves us so much (John 3:16). If Jesus Himself, came to this earth to suffer and die for me, what makes me think I am exempt from suffering?

By no means am I saying Anna Benton is a punishment for my sins, or that she is causing me to suffer. I would choose her a million times over, without pause, without hesitation. Not to sound cliché, but I love her so much, it hurts. She and Baker are pieces of my heart, living outside of my body, and I love them with all of my being. It's just that I had spent most of her existence pouting. To be honest, I had spent almost *my* entire life pouting. And for what? Because my childhood wasn't picture-perfect? Because life didn't turn out like I planned? Because it was hard? Because we had not gotten a diagnosis yet?

While I sometimes struggle as I navigate through my far from typical life, every difficulty I have faced is miniscule compared to what Jesus did for me.

It wasn't until I read Morgan Cheek's <u>On Milk and Honey</u>, I had the sobering revelation that it's not about me. Reading her eloquent account of raising twin daughters with special needs and finding God's goodness in unexpected places changed my life. Her book, along with the scriptures she quotes, are life giving. So much of her journey is similar to mine and while some parts of her book were like pouring salt in my wounds, other parts were absolutely freeing.

Have you ever read something that made you feel like someone had heard your thoughts? Thoughts you've kept to yourself and not shared with anyone? That's God, my friends!

After reading it, I felt reaffirmed in my purpose and was given a new perspective. Morgan spoke on patience and joy found in waiting and the unknown. That can apply to those waiting for a significant other, a baby, a diagnosis, etc. It's all about keeping your eyes on God and trusting that His plan is bigger than our own. Her book was so refreshing and helped fade my "me, me, me" mentality.

Everyone faces challenges; they just might look differently for one person than another. And I would guess, other people don't pout about them as much as I sometimes do.

Hearing Mercy Me's "Even If" caused a pivotal moment in my life as well. That song says everything I couldn't. Every word touched my heart and I wouldn't do it justice without quoting some of it:

> I know You're able and I know You can
> Save through the fire with Your mighty hand
> But even if You don't
> my hope is You alone…
> But God, when you choose
> To leave mountains unmovable
> Give me the strength to be able to sing
> It is well with my soul

Some days are harder than I can bear, as if life were a boiling pot filled with events that caused the temperature and pressure to rise to the point of eventually boiling over and shooting the top straight to the ceiling. Anna Benton has an extremely rare genetic condition and we make choices every day to help improve her care and quality of life. Some days are amazing and some days chip away at my soul. We have always tried to praise the Lord during the bad times and not just the good. However, I've always had this lingering question of why

God hasn't completely healed her. I have faith that He can. I know He can. I just wondered sometimes why He hasn't yet.

That song helped me come to the realization that it's not necessarily my business to know why the Lord put me on this path. It's my business to praise Him anyway. Even if Anna Benton never takes a step in her life, I will praise Him anyway. She is my beautiful, goofy, strong willed, curly headed, million-dollar smiling, Daddy's look-a-like little angel. And I'm beyond grateful she's mine.

While we have daily challenges (who doesn't?), the Lord is working something mighty in our lives. He allows us to feel sorrow in order to mold us into what He needs us to be (2 Corinthians 7:10). Romans 8:32 says, "He who did not spare His own son but gave Him up for us all, how will He not also with Him, graciously give us all things?"

Our "far from typical life" that I often speak of has yielded so many blessings and has given me a pretty spectacular platform to speak of God's goodness. I mean, that's our purpose in life anyways, right? We are to be the salt and light (Matthew 5:13–16) and to glorify God, no matter our circumstances. God is good.

Like Daniel 3:18 depicts, even during challenging times, God "is still good." Shadrach, Meshach, and Abednego were tested and thrown into the fiery furnace, but the Lord protected them from harm. Now, I'm not saying that having a child with special needs could be compared to a fiery furnace, but it is a challenge, nonetheless. We may be tested daily, but God is protecting us from harm and He is still good.

And we know that all things work together for good to them that love God, to them who are the called according to his purpose.
—Romans 8:28

CHAPTER

Determined for "Normal"

God hasn't invited us into a disorderly, unkempt life, but into something holy and beautiful—as beautiful on the inside as the outside.
—Shauna Niequist (The message of 1 Thessalonians 4:7)

If you are always trying to be normal, you will
never know how amazing you can be.
—Maya Angelou

Do not be conformed to this world, but be transformed by the renewal
of your mind, that by testing you may discern what is the will of
God, what is good and acceptable and perfect. —Romans 12:2

Merriam-Webster's dictionary defines the word *normal* as "conforming to a type, standard, or regular pattern." In the world of special needs, the word *normal* is heard often, somewhat as an antagonist to activities of daily life (ADLs) and as a measurement of a child's disability. I, personally, have a love/hate relationship with it.

Therapy paperwork, preschool applications, and insurance forms all have something in common, besides the fact that they are painstakingly long: they all want to know your child's abilities. For some, a lot of those forms can be quickly completed by checking "N/A." But for moms like me, there is usually not enough space on the lines to hold all of the information I need to provide about my child(ren).

Anna Benton's required level of care resembles that of a four-month-old. She is globally developmentally delayed, non-ambulatory, and nonverbal. She is unable to feed or clothe herself and requires assistance with all ADLs. She is considered a "total care patient" in the world of pediatric medicine—the opposite of most children her age.

In a pediatric course I took as a new nurse, I remember the instructor saying the word *normal* wasn't received well from the special needs community. When speaking to a parent, it can have a negative connotation and implies that their child is viewed as *abnormal*. Instead, we should use the word *typical*, as it suggests more of a behavior than an ability.

While Anna Benton is not like a typical child her age, I want her to have as many of the typical childhood experiences that we have all had. I loved swimming, watching cartoons, going to amusement parks, and eating popsicles outside in the summer. She may be developmentally delayed and physically handicapped but she is able to enjoy all of those things. She *loves* water and giggles the entire time we're at the pool! Our version of enjoyment may look a little different but I can assure you, we have fun just the same.

We had been hermits the first year after having Anna Benton while we became accustomed to all of the changes that were taking place. But once we got comfortable with our new routine, we were ready for life to get back to normal. *There's that word again...*

I had been a SAHM for almost a year and the Lord placed an opportunity in front of me. A medical daycare for children with special needs was coming to our area and they were looking to hire pediatric nurses on staff. (If that's not a God thing, I don't know what is!) After a phone call and a meeting with the owner, Anna Benton was taken on as their first patient and I was hired as the Administrator.

I was so excited to have the opportunity to work again. Not only that, I was able to bring her with me every day. God was orchestrating everything perfectly.

Once I started having an income and we weren't living on that tight budget anymore, I was even more determined for us to provide typical childhood experiences for the kids. I had also decided that if I couldn't buy dance costumes and dollhouses, Anna Benton was going to be the best dressed kid in the room! That may have been my silly way of compensating for not being able to do all of the typical things a mom of a toddler gets to do, but oh well. Coping mechanisms, right?

We had big elaborate birthday parties for the kids with over the top decorations and fabulous cakes. I invited Baker's school friends and patients from Anna Benton's daycare. We also took a trip to Disney World that year. (I'm not sure who had more fun, Justin and I, or the kids.) It's like I was trying to cram in as much fun and *normal* as possible.

Anytime our friends invited us to events, we were there, even if that meant I was packing our Suburban full of equipment, medications, and supplies for Anna Benton. I didn't want us to miss out on anything and I was terrified someone would be disappointed if we weren't there. I carted that poor child all over creation and looking back, it would have probably been in her best interest to have stayed home with a sitter sometimes.

This kept on for quite a while and I was wearing myself out. One of the most ridiculous things we ever did was take her to an outdoor Independence Day celebration. We had never been to this particular event before. We planned to meet our friends before it started but it took us longer to pack up our *house* than we anticipated. (Princess Anna Benton requires her chariot and *lots* of accessories.)

We pretty much had to go off-roading to find parking (a mile away) and the stroller we brought for her wasn't built for such terrain. Justin ended up carrying her most of the way while I drug the stroller behind me, bouncing the whole way there. Baker wasn't exactly thrilled about walking that far either. And may I remind you, this was in the midst of the Mississippi summer heat and humidity.

By the time we found our friends, we were pouring sweat and exhausted. The kids loved the picnic blankets, fans, fireworks, and music, but Justin and I were dreading the trek back. It took us even longer to get back than it did to get there. We decided on that *very* long walk back to the car, that we needed to do our homework before getting ourselves into anything like that again.

It wasn't until I bought tickets for a Mommy and Me Princess Tea that I realized I needed to truly rethink my determination for *normal*. I had been looking forward to it and this was going to be a chance for me to do something with her that I had dreamt of, long before she arrived. The week before the tea, we found ourselves in the hospital again for breakthrough seizures and by the time Anna Benton was discharged, we were worn out. I didn't feel like dressing up the next day and she needed to rest. We both did.

Bless her, she had little sores on her head from having an EEG that resembled something like Frankenstein, and I wasn't in the mood to explain anything if a stranger asked. Justin and I decided it would be best for us to sit this one out. My feelings were hurt that we had to miss it but I knew that it was in both of our best interests to stay home. That was one pass I gave myself that I will never regret.

Looking back, there were so many times I over-extended myself, all because I wanted to *feel* normal. Why was I doing this? What was I proving to anyone? What was I proving to myself? That I was strong? That I could save face? That we could rise above our circumstances?

Our friends and family would completely understand if we couldn't come to something or if we had to leave early, but I didn't want to miss out on anything. I also didn't want someone to think we were struggling. I was so committed to proving that I could handle anything. But even if I was showing up to birthday parties, play dates, or dinners, it was only a fragmented version of me. My determined-to-be-normal shell was there but the inside was tired and weary, with a dash of occasional bitterness mixed in.

Looking back, there are probably tons of moments of connection with family and friends missed due to only my shell being present.

After a few mistakes and some heart-to-hearts, we learned to be selective with where we take Anna Benton. At the same time, we learned to divide and conquer so Baker wouldn't have to miss something if Anna Benton couldn't go. Justin and I now have it down to a science on who stays with her and who goes with him, depending on the event. Everyone is much happier this way and it sure beats feeling like we're moving every time we leave the house.

8

CHAPTER

Isolation

For just as the body is one and has many members, and all the
members of the body, though many, are one body, so it is with Christ.
—1 Corinthians 12:12

I've heard there's a fine line between a hero and a lunatic. I guess
you could say the same for the balance between my need for
"normal" versus my need for peace—there's a fine line.

Justin and I were breaking our necks to keep from missing out
on anything. Because we were exhausting ourselves, we tried to take
things down a few notches, allow ourselves some grace, and missed
out on a few things (birthday parties, family meals, etc.).

Unfortunately, that became too easy and saying "No" and "I'm
sorry, we can't make it" became second language for us. I decided
it was easier for us to disappoint people on the front end by saying
no, than commit to going somewhere and have to back out at the
last minute, or leave early because of Anna Benton. That became a
habit and we started finding ourselves missing more events than we
attended.

While it was easier to stay home instead of packing the whole house to go somewhere, we were missing out on the feeling of community we loved so much. We missed time with our family, friends, and our church. We found ourselves isolated from the outside world—our own fault, not anyone else's.

Home felt safe and it became harder and harder to leave. On bad days, it was easier for me to shut the world out. Sometimes, I didn't feel like explaining a new symptom or new medication to anyone. Justin and I would talk about it at length and I didn't have the energy to explain it any further.

It wasn't that we wanted to keep secrets from our family and friends; we were just shielding ourselves from further hurt. It wasn't always easy answering questions like: "Well have you tried this?" "Who's her doctor? So and So goes to Dr. So and So, and they already have a diagnosis." "Do you think it's something in your breastmilk?" "Don't you think it's time to get a second opinion?" "Why is all of that testing taking so long?" I literally could go on and on…

Listening to it was exhausting. Explaining it was almost always out of the question. It felt like life was being drained out of me as I tried to keep my composure during these types of interrogations. We felt judged, as if we were negligent parents who weren't doing enough for our child. It got to the point that we both started dreading phone calls. We knew they all meant well; we dreaded them nonetheless.

And those feelings of isolation spilled over into everyday life as well. We have missed many playdates and trips to the park because of our lives revolving around appointments. If there was an off-chance that our schedules aligned with a friend's, I then had to face the choice of carrying Anna Benton or strolling her (if the locations was handicap accessible). We have also been invited somewhere to find that there are no handicap accessible restrooms or changing tables, forcing me to have to change her diaper in the back of our car. Splash pads and jump houses aren't really an option for her so we have to bring accommodations for her with us. See why we pack up and bring the house?

While I definitely don't want to make it seem like we are burdened; I just want to shed light that being a parent of a child with special needs has a lot of challenges—many unanticipated, and especially by the outside world. That can definitely make you feel like you're fighting a battle alone.

The older our children get, the less I'm finding our schedules match and our paths cross. As discouraging as that can sometimes feel, I'm so thankful my friends don't allow me to isolate myself too much. They get me out of the house, even if it means they have to force me sometimes. Some of my best friends know how stubborn I am, so they've learned not to take no for answer. Bless them!

While I tried to shut myself off from the outside world, there were also plenty of times that I just needed a few minutes to myself—away from my family too. (Remember my Klove jam sessions? Yeah, those were still happening and I added trips to Menchies in the mix. Fro-yo fixes everything, right?) I would be so emotionally and mentally drained that I needed time away from medicines, feeding schedules, and diaper changes. Those 5–30 minutes I took for myself helped bring a little sanity to the chaos.

Justin and I sometimes went into auto-pilot to get stuff done around the house and get the kids taken care of. I was usually in bed by the time the kids were in bed and I certainly didn't have the energy for anything else (if you get my drift)… But that can only go on so long before you start feeling more like roommates instead of spouses. I mean, have you seen the divorce rates of couples with a child with special needs? Yikes!

By no means am I saying that Justin and I have ever considered divorce; I'm just saying that it is imperative that we don't isolate ourselves, especially from each other. We should give our spouse the best part of ourselves, and not just what's left over from our day.

The Lord tells us, "Come with me by yourselves to a quiet place and get some rest" (Mark 6:31). While it is important for us to have quiet time with Him, I think I was taking that "by yourselves" a little too far... He didn't intend for us to completely seclude ourselves. Instead, it is important for us to have community and fellowship

(Hebrews 10:24–25), "for the body does not consist of one member but of many" (1 Corinthians 12:14).

I craved Sunday mornings, especially time with our Lifegroup. But I really needed worship hour. Yes, there were times I wished there was a direct door to *my* pew (a Southern Baptist thing) and an escape hatch in an attempt avoid well-meant questions. But, I craved having time around a hundred other believers, all singing and worshipping together.

Like He said, "where two or more are gathered in My name, there shall I be also" (Matthew 18:20). At some of my lowest points, when I did well to get myself up and out of the house, that's when the Lord met me right there in *my* pew. And I'm pretty sure it's been soaked with a few extra ounces of tears since Anna Benton was born.

But I am here to tell you, some of the finest people I know are ones I've met through our church. They have loved our family and prayed us through our hardest times. They've sent food, cards of encouragement, and helped with Baker while Justin and I were in the hospital with Anna Benton. They are all so accommodating to our family and the preschool director still allows her to be in the nursery, even though she's four years old.

My point in all of this, is that isolation can feel like everyone else around you is moving while you're sitting still. They seem to progress while we seem stagnant. It can sometimes be easy to focus on our differences, but thank God, our friends and church try hard not to allow us to do so. It takes effort on both sides and we are beyond grateful for their willingness to include us, despite our need for accommodations for our little princess.

Goodness, I'm so grateful I didn't miss out on such wonderful friendships because I was too busy isolating myself. It has taken us quite a while to find balance between being hermits and social butterflies but I think for the most part, we've learned a pretty decent compromise. After all, we gave up on *normal* a long time ago!

CHAPTER

The Answer

Since, then, you have been raised with Christ, set your hearts
on things above, where Christ is, seated at the right hand of
God. Set your minds on things above, not on earthly things.
—Colossians 3:1–2

I have spoken previously about being a bit of a control freak. Let me elaborate a touch. I am classic Type A personality. I'm a little competitive and I like to be in charge—it's in my DNA. I was captain of the dance team and president of Astra club while in high school. I was a charge nurse in the pediatric ER and I was eventually hired as the administrator of a medical daycare. While strong willed, I am a "yes man" by nature. I wouldn't go as far as to say I am a people pleaser, but I do like my people happy. I had a *need* to be well liked and unfortunately, I thought I had an image to uphold. (Thank you, Lord, for grace.)

Even though Justin and I had been thrown some curveballs in the last few years, we always seemed to regroup and push forward well. He had moved up to supervisor in his department and the medical daycare's business was booming. I joined the local Junior League and became a member of the Mississippi Epilepsy Foundation board. Days were filled with work, appointments and therapies for the kids, marketing, volunteering, and so on. Nights were filled with laundry, dinners, and homework. My cell phone was constantly ringing from appointment reminders, texts from employees, and calls from parents. My schedule looked like an air traffic control switchboard—so many dots everywhere. On paper, I looked amazing but to say that I was burning the candle at both ends would be an understatement.

During all of the chaos, Anna Benton was still undergoing genetic testing. We had gotten to the point that we were joking that whatever she had would be so rare that it wouldn't even have a name, just letters and numbers. Because her condition is considered extremely rare, she was invited to be a part of a research study through the National Institute of Health (NIH) in Bethesda, Maryland. This study specifically involves children with congenital hand anomalies. Through the study, the NIH covered the cost of whole exome sequencing (WES), a test that could find variances with Anna Benton's DNA, versus mine and Justin's.

If we had chosen to do WES privately instead of through the research study, it would cost upwards of five thousand dollars. That's right, FIVE THOUSAND DOLLARS!

It all sounded wonderful so we were ready to get signed up. We were very hopeful that it (WES) would yield answers because after all, it's being run by the NIH. If anyone could find a diagnosis for an extremely rare condition, it had to be them! We were told it could take up to six months to run the test and we tried our best to not think about it every day (another coping mechanism used in an attempt to make time pass by more quickly).

In the meantime, Anna Benton's genetics doctor left the children's hospital for another job out of state. I was so discouraged because we were yet again, feeling like we were on the cusp of progress, all to have the rug swept out from under our feet.

We met with a new genetics doctor, one who was very confident and brash. (I'll explain.) She recommended we have WES done through the hospital in addition to the NIH's research study. In a not-nice-way, she asked why we had not already done that. What she didn't speak, I can assure you, was said with her facial expression. I explained that we were told the test was not guaranteed to yield results, nor would insurance cover its costs. (Not everyone has five grand, just lying around). She seemed less than empathetic, urging that the results would come back sooner and that it would be worth our cost. While I wasn't impressed with her attitude or looks of judgement, she had a point. I mean, that's what we have been wanting all of this time, right? A diagnosis?

After conversations of budget cuts and working overtime to cover costs, Justin and I decided to have the additional WES done. And because Anna Benton had lost some milestones (elaboration to follow), a follow up magnetic resonance image (MRI) was ordered in addition to the WES.

At one point, Anna Benton was babbling and saying "Mama" and "Dada" and then eventually, just stopped. Her doctors couldn't explain why she lost that milestone but felt there was something structurally to blame. It had been almost two years since her last MRI so a new finding was expected. (Let me tell you, hearing both of my children's first words were some of the most incredible moments of my life. My heart stung at the thought of never hearing Anna Benton speak again. I was determined to find a reason for her regression and hopefully, a solution.) Once again, more hope, more lab work, and more imaging followed.

A couple of days after Anna Benton's MRI, we had not heard anything yet. While at work, I left a message with the genetics department because I *needed* to know the results. I found myself back in that Mama Bear mode, on the edge of having a panic attack.

Her genetics doctor called me back late that afternoon with some pretty devastating news. The MRI showed "progressive cerebellar atrophy" and a variant consistent with Dandy Walker syndrome. The doctor explained that she doesn't have Dandy Walker but was concerned because her cerebellum had atrophied (shrunk) so much, so quickly. She also explained that this could be the reason for lost milestones and is consistent with her vision abnormalities, coordination issues, hypertonic (stiff) extremities, and lack of gross motor development.

To this day, the end of our phone conversation is still a blur. My mind was spinning from the second I heard the word "progressive" and I was ready to start researching. I hope I told her goodbye before I hung up the phone…

Immediately after my conversation with the doctor, I called Justin. I usually try to de-medicalatize (I know that's not a real word) the news he hears (not because he is not strong enough to handle it but more because I don't want him to worry as much as I do), but my mind had gone off the deep end this time. My heart was broken and I wasn't able to filter what I told him. I can't imagine what he felt as his nurse of a wife, the one who is typically composed, was spewing word vomit to him about his daughter. I probably made the situation seem hopeless and as expected after my dramatic presentation, he too was broken hearted and overwhelmed.

I was in no condition to be at work for the remainder of the day so I scooped up Anna Benton and headed home to fall apart. I just held her and rocked her, shedding every tear I had left in my body. I was terrified and begged God for mercy. I couldn't switch my spinning brain off to listen to my heart. My wheels were turning and my heart was aching.

I couldn't (and still can't) imagine her becoming so sickly and frail from a *progressive* disease process. The idea of possibly having to bury her one day took my breath away. It still sometimes keeps me up at night—it would any parent. I try not to think about it and it's best for me to not let my mind go there. Like a friend once told me, "falling in the water doesn't make you drown, *staying* there does."

The next few days and weeks were difficult. It was hard to break the news to family and friends. I wanted so badly to stay composed as we told them, to keep the situation from becoming one big tear-fest. Some were easier to tell than others and some, we didn't want to tell at all. (I can't tell you how important it is to have a strong support system. I thank God for them!)

Within a matter of weeks from having a second WES, Anna Benton's genetics counselor called. She asked if I was driving and at the time, I was. She told me to call her back when I had a minute but at that point, I knew she was calling about something important and there was *no way* I was getting off the phone with her!

She did in fact, have some important news. She had lab results and more importantly, a diagnosis! That's right, a DIAGNOSIS!

After over two full years of genetic testing, lab work, imaging, hope, despair, frustration, and tears, the answer that we had longed for had finally come.

It turns out, the information received from Anna Benton's MRI was just as vital as the lab work that had been done. Once cerebellar atrophy had been plugged into the genetic database (I hope I'm describing this correctly) along with her lab work results, a connection was found. The pieces of the puzzle had *finally* come together!

Anna Benton was diagnosed with CACNA1G gene mutation on Chromosome 17. I always said it was going to be a bunch of letters and numbers. That's exactly what it is. It is a spontaneous and dominant mutation on one tiny chromosome which is responsible for all of her symptoms (seizures, polysyndactyly, stiff extremities, vision abnormalities) and developmental delays.

Our genetics counselor was so excited to *finally* be able to give us the diagnosis we had been long awaiting and I couldn't wait to call Justin. This phone conversation full of news would be much better than our last.

Immediately, I was ready to start googling but I had been warned that because Anna Benton's condition was so rare, I probably wouldn't find much on the internet about it. I had also been told that WES is still fairly new and yields much more data than anyone has the capability of understanding. And that was exactly the case.

There was barely a word about her condition on the internet and what *was* available, would take someone far more educated than me to understand. I had spent hours looking up research articles and digging for facts but I wasn't making much progress.

There is no telling how much data I burned through, on my phone that month. Thank goodness for my husband and his willingness to sign us up for the unlimited plan!

I can't help but look back at all of that (my relentless researching and *need* for a diagnosis) and smile. That precious diagnosis that we had been desperately chasing was finally found. But, we were no further along than before we had gotten it. Sure, there was a sense of peace and closure that came with it. There was even more comfort in knowing that there is a less than one percent chance of Baker having it (some children are reported to become symptomatic later in life) or our future children having it. But still, the diagnosis had not proven to be as quintessential as we thought. That is just another example of me putting more faith in the field of medicine than God. (Thank you, Lord, for grace.) It is more important for me to keep my sights on Him and not on worldly things—like that precious diagnosis (Colossians 3:2).

I wouldn't be telling the truth if I said it was all a piece of cake after Anna Benton was diagnosed. Praise God, her treatment didn't change because they had been properly treating her symptoms the whole time. But something changed within me and Justin and I know exactly why. It was hearing the word "progressive" with her MRI results. It was like we started falsely accepting that Anna Benton's best had already come and gone (speaking then stopping) and we were headed down a hard road for the remainder of her life. (Praise the Lord, that's not the case!)

It set a fire in me to be grateful for the time we have with her and to stop sweating the small stuff. Justin was ready to increase our life insurance and draw up our will. He's a finance and details kind of guy and his wheels were spinning. He started preparing for the kids if something happened to us before they became adults. He also started looking at long term care facilities for the handicapped, in case Baker wouldn't be able to care for Anna Benton once we're gone.

Watching him process all of that broke my heart, but it also made me love him even more. He has always provided so well for our family and it was touching, watching a precious father plan for his children.

But isn't that what God does? He's our heavenly Father and He has already planned what is best for us.

'For I know the plans I have for you,' declares the Lord. 'Plans to prosper you and not to harm you, plans to give you hope and a future.'
—Jeremiah 29:11

10

CHAPTER

Steel Magnolia

She is clothed in strength and dignity, and she
laughs without fear of the future.
—Proverbs 31:25

Anyone who knows me very well, knows that my favorite movie is <u>Steel Magnolias.</u> I can quote it in its entirety, and when my family gets together, we have been known to bring it up a time or *three*. On any given day, I may break out a "I like pink. Pink is my signature color" or "It looks like two pigs fightin' under a blanket" or "If you don't have something nice to say, come sit by me" occasionally. Justin has learned to accept it, expect it, and bless his heart, he loves me in spite of it. (If you haven't seen it, please remedy that as quickly as possible!)

The characters in that movie are fantastic and I practically idolized them as a kid. I would love to say that I act like M'Lynn, reserved wife and mother extraordinaire, or like Truvy, always caring and neighborly. But the older I get, the more I act like Ouiser, sassy and filter-less. Again, bless my sweet husband…

I think I was destined to love this movie because these women embodied Southern Christian culture and remind me of so many of the women I grew up around. Plus, my Gladys and Ouiser have a lot in common; I think we would all be best friends in real life.

The name "Steel Magnolias" comes from Robert Harling's play. It is based on a true story of his sister's life, a diabetic who faced multiple trials with a strong, supportive group of women by her side. Not only is the title fitting, it means "delicate as a magnolia, but tough as steel."

If there is a term that defines Anna Benton Coleman, it is a steel magnolia! While she may be considered medically fragile, that child is tough as nails and has endured more in her short little life than many of us will go through in a lifetime. And she does it all with a smile on her face. She's incredible and she's my hero.

From infancy, she had a way of lighting up the room. Friends and family visited us in the hospital, expecting to see a sickly, frail little baby. Instead, they found a silly, little giggly girl, who just rolled with the punches. She was hooked to monitors, IV pumps, and an EEG machine. She has been radiated from enough x-rays, CTs, and MRIs, that she ought to glow in the dark. Instead of how most of us would act through all of that, she found most of her experiences quite hilarious. We were all inspired by her resilience (to this day, we still are) and that's when I started calling her my little Steel Magnolia.

Anna Benton has changed my life for the better. She may be nonverbal but she has such a good attitude and an infectious personality. When she smiles, she smiles with her whole face. When she laughs, she laughs with her whole body. That sweet giggle of hers could make my heart explode. She loves music and goes nuts when she's held and danced around. You can't help but smile and laugh with her. She loves Baker and thinks everything he does is wonderful. She acts the same way about her Daddy. It just melts this Mama's heart watching them and the way they love each other.

There are so many times I just look at her in awe. I get lost in her big green eyes shaded by beautifully long eyelashes. There is something magical that shines through them out into her world. There is a pureness and innocence about her, like a God given vision of love and a picture of heaven. I wish I could bottle that pure joy up and drink it. She is truly amazing and I'm so grateful she's mine.

Having her reminds me of the meaning of grace. I am a sinner, saved by grace through faith in Jesus Christ (Ephesians 2:8). While I deserve nothing, God has blessed me beyond measure anyways. Without her, I may have never truly appreciated grace or even come to fully understand it. She has awakened a part of me that helped change my attitude from one of entitlement to one of gratitude.

Proverbs 24:16 says, "For a righteous man may fall seven times, and rises again; but the wicked stumble in the time of calamity." Because of Anna Benton's diagnoses and developmental delays, I have been given multiple opportunities to stumble. And stumble, I have. It is easy to get overwhelmed with the responsibilities of raising a child with special needs. But because of her resilience and sweet laughter, as well as strength from the Lord, I am able to "rise again." Being her Mama has been one of the most challenging and terrifying things I've ever done, but by far, it is one of the most rewarding.

I sometimes get the impression that Justin and I are pitied. Some people act like we deserve some sort of medal for taking care of her. When people apologize to us for having to go through so much, I usually tell them that we are fine. We're simply doing what it takes to take care of our baby girl. They would do the same if they were given the same opportunity. And I say opportunity because she is amazing and I promise, we don't need sympathy.

Prayers? Yes. Sympathy? No.

One of the bright sides to Anna Benton's delays is that she is blissfully unaware of anything except what's right in front of her. She doesn't realize she has had a hard row to hoe, because she is unable to compare her life to someone else's. When she goes through a painful procedure, she may cry at the time. But within minutes of being given her favorite toy and a cuddle, she is back to her giggly self; as if she had never hurt at all. Wouldn't it be wonderful if we were all like that? I'm telling you, she's amazing!

I remember so clearly when she was having her first video EEG. Video EEGs are a little more intense than a regular EEG and can last several days (in order to catch a seizure that may be missed with a shorter EEG). The leads are actually glued in place to her head and by the time the tech is done placing all of them (at least 30), everyone in the room usually has a buzz because the smell of the glue is so strong. I was told most children cry during that process; but not my AB. She thought it was hilarious. Every time the tech dried the glue using a special tube connected to an air supply, it would make a funny noise and Anna Benton would laugh so hard that she couldn't catch her breath. In fact, she had us *all* laughing.

After the tech was finished, she wrapped Anna Benton's head with gauze to keep all of the leads in place. After a quick shower, I had put on my glasses and wrapped a towel around my wet hair. I realized we looked like twins with our fabulous matching glasses and headwraps, so I snapped a quick pic. It makes me smile every time I see it because it reminds me of how easy it is to make her smile and how important it is for me to keep a sense of humor. There I was with no make-up, a wet towel on my head, glasses, and an Ole Miss t-shirt to boot—not exactly looking like the picture of beauty, but it's still one of my favorite photos of me and my baby girl.

Speaking of a sense of humor, I'm reminded of the day of Baker's kindergarten play and graduation. Justin and I sometimes joke that we are the definition of Murphy's law: "Whatever can go wrong, will." Murphy's Law is a great summation of that day. Allow me to elaborate.

Baker was a disciple in his play and he had worked hard practicing his lines and song. Anna Benton had been sick for a couple of days prior but woke up afebrile and acting fine that morning. I was determined not to miss my little disciple sing and I felt brave enough to bring Anna Benton with me (that was cute). So out the door, we all went.

We sat in the back of the auditorium in case she had a surprise in store. As Baker and his classmates walked in, dressed in adorably cute costumes, I was able to show him where we were sitting and made sure to let him know which direction to face when he sang. This

Mama was ready for her baby boy's time to shine. Sister, however, had other plans...

The surprise I prepared for by sitting in the back of the room was nothing compared to the surprise she had in mind. I was thinking a fussy spell or something of the sort but that wasn't the case. She had a blowout sitting in my lap while we were watching Baker sing. I had white pants on. The gym smelled like death and Justin had to clean my chair with a pack of antibacterial wipes I had in my purse. It felt like chaos. I scooped her up and carried her out of the gym as I felt said blowout running down my pants leg. There was no changing table in the restroom so I had to change her on the counter by the sinks; a space that is less than a foot wide. It was a disaster but I managed to get her cleaned up and her clothes changed just in time for her to poop again. By that point, I was beyond flustered.

Then I looked up. There I was, in the middle of a poop nightmare, covered from my waist to my knees, smelling absolutely horrendous. As I stood there in front of that mirror, I died out laughing. I couldn't help myself! It was so bad, it was comical!

There was no way I could walk back into that gym looking and smelling like that so I decided to take us home. Ultimately, I missed the end of Baker's play and watching him walk across the stage to receive his diploma. My feelings were terribly hurt but the more the events of that morning played through my mind, the more comical they became. If there was any situation that Murphy's law described, that was it! Anna Benton had pooped all over me and my chair. There was no changing table. She had pooped again before I got her to the car. I had to change her in the car. I had no clothes to change into. I left my phone in the gym. Justin had no idea that I went home. I missed Baker's graduation. Justin had circled the building several times looking for us. It was a mess and it *all* went wrong. Thanks, Murphy...

That morning may have been a train wreck but we ended up having ourselves a good laugh, mostly at my expense. Afterward, we all sat together and watched the video Justin took of Baker graduating. The tears of pride fell just the same as if I had been sitting there in person. In that moment, I was reminded of grace; to allow myself some in times like these, and for the grace of Baker's understanding of why I couldn't be there the for the end.

I'm sure all mothers have experienced chaos like that a time or two. But Anna Benton sure has some tricks up her sleeves at what seems like the most inopportune times. That little *stinker...* Get it?

She may have some surprises for me often but I can't imagine life without her. Because of her, Justin and I became a part of a totally different world that we never knew existed— the world of special needs parenting. Sure, I had been exposed to it as a pediatric nurse, but never had a true appreciation for it until Anna Benton came along.

To be honest, I was a little intimidated by all of the Mama and Papa Bears I met throughout my nursing career. But, now that I have a child who needs advocation, I *totally* get it. (Pediatric Nursing 101: Always listen to parents. They are invaluable and know *way* more about their child than you!)

Anna Benton is also the reason for my introduction into a tribe of some pretty fabulous moms; strong women (who make me look like a feeble snowflake) who move mountains for their children. They accepted me and my family into their community with open arms and open hearts. They have become dear friends. Our children's' abilities may vary greatly but they have been a wonderful support group and resource for my family. They too, are steel magnolias.

I know our lives would look totally different without our Anna Benton, and that makes me all the more grateful that God gave her to us. I know I've said it before, but I have to say it again. She changed me. Because of her, I learned that nothing else matters besides relying on and trusting God, while walking by faith and not by sight (2 Corinthians 5:7).

I look at life through a totally different set of lenses because of her. I try to not sweat the small stuff. I try to allow myself some grace as well as extend it to others. I am now much more grateful for my blessings. I have more compassion as a nurse, for my patients and their families. And lastly, I try to keep a sense of humor, even amongst the chaos. Because if she can laugh, so can I.

11

CHAPTER

Much Needed Rest

For I know the plans I have for you, declares the Lord, plans for welfare and not for evil, to give you a future and a hope. Then you will call upon me and come and pray to me, and I will hear you. You will seek me and find me when you seek me with all your heart. I will be found by you, declares the Lord, and I will restore your fortunes and gather you from all the nations and all the places where I have driven you, declares the Lord, and I will bring you back to the place from which I sent you into exile.
—Jeremiah 29:11–14

The older I get and the older my children get, the more I have learned to value family. My priorities starting changing after having Baker and they *really* changed after Anna Benton entered our world. That busy schedule and life that I was determined to lead were stressing me out and making me miss out on what was important. I was becoming miserable.

Management started feeling like a never-ending hamster wheel. As soon as I would hop on, fix one problem, then hop off, another one would need *fixing* shortly after. And right back on the wheel,

I got. And after a workday full of putting out "fires," I came home having to put out a few more. There was always laundry to be done or counters to be cleaned.

I was showing up to work and marketing events frazzled and worn down. I was working forty to sixty hours a week and answering emails, texts, and calls at night. I was trying to cram so much into a day that could only hold twenty-four hours of what I needed to put into it. That's on top of Baker's weekly OT and Anna Benton's regular weekly therapies and monthly specialty appointments.

I wasn't sleeping well at night, if at all. I would cope with sarcasm and snarky subtleties like having a sign in my office that said, "Every day I'm hustling" and a coffee mug that said, "Y'all need Jesus." (That is still one of my favorite mugs but I need to take a Sharpie and replace "Y'all" with "I.")

I used to envy Justin for being able to fall asleep at the drop of a hat, whether he was in the car, on the couch, or in public. Because I wasn't sleeping well at night, I became the one napping all of the time—I'm talking in therapy waiting rooms and dozing in Baker's carpool line. I had frequent headaches, chest pain, and stomach ulcers. My face looked like I had just hit puberty. I was burnt out, stressed out, and spiritually empty.

Why was this all so hard? God had handcrafted this opportunity for this wonderful medical daycare, a place for Anna Benton to attend and a place for me to work. Constantly thinking that I was supposed to be there is what kept me there so long; that, and the fact that I absolutely loved helping families like ours. It was an honor caring for those sweet babies and their parents but I stressed myself out if everything wasn't perfect all of the time.

Justin and I often talked about how hard things had gotten. We have never really been a couple that argued. We're more of the silent treatment type. I'm not saying that's the way to handle things either—that's just how we roll. But during that time, we had ourselves some doozies of arguments.

I had been in management for almost two years and instead of getting easier, it was getting harder. My plans were starting to feel like they weren't the Lord's plans. I felt like I was struggling to have the mental stability to manage Anna Benton's care along with a daycare facility, patients, their families, and staff. I had been going at 100 mph for too long, and I was beyond worn down.

There were so many times I tried to cope with my circumstances by going into somewhat of an autopilot mode, almost feeling numb at times. It was easier for me to power through some difficulties rather than deal with real emotion. As a parent, and especially a parent of a child with special needs, a lot of my day-to-day activities are easier to get done in auto-pilot mode. Feed here, medicate there. Flush here, change there. But I can honestly say, that is no way to live.

I came across Colossians 3:23 while searching for God's words about time management. It says, "whatever you do, work at it with all your heart, as working for the Lord, not for human masters." How profound! I was doing the exact opposite of what that scripture commands. I was serving too many masters and trying to please too many people. I also found 1 Corinthians 10:31 saying, "So whether you eat or drink or whatever you do, do it all for the glory of God." I was only giving half of an effort to most of what I was involved in because I was spreading myself too thin—at work, in my social life, and at home. I also wasn't doing everything for God's glory; it was probably for more of my own. I was burned out and used up.

I was reminded of Jonah and how God sent a storm over his boat. It took that storm and three days in a whale's belly before he decided to obey and head the direction the Lord was leading him to go. I had felt the *storm* for a while but I was stubborn and had fought to stay long enough.

After a lot of prayer and some long, civil talks with Justin, we realized it was time for me to step down from management. It took me too long to come to that decision because like I said, it's in my DNA to lead. Also, I'm stubborn. I had been terrified for so many reasons about leaving and I didn't want to disappoint anyone. I had always risen, never taking a step back. But the Lord was placing it on my heart that it was time to rest, humble myself, remove the chaos, and put *my* family before everyone else's.

Tears were rolling down my cheeks as I was writing my resignation letter. Though extremely stressful, I had loved this job. I loved my staff, I loved my patients, I loved their families, and I really loved having Anna Benton with me every day. But, it was time to let go of my fears and trust that God's plan was bigger than my own.

I may have been tearful as I resigned but as the words left my lips, it was as if a tremendous weight was lifted. I had an overwhelming, Godly sense of peace wash over me followed by one of the best night's sleep of my entire life. My previous inhibitions were left in that office that day and I was ready to take the next step, completely trusting the Lord and what He had planned.

Little did I know, the Lord was again working something mighty in our lives. My previous nurse manager in the pediatric ER had known how much I was struggling to balance home and work life. She was not surprised when she heard I resigned from management and seemed eager to have me back. She knew I needed freedom because of Anna Benton and her schedule and was more than willing to provide that flexibility.

My return to the ER was seamless and I have to give credit where credit is due. It was all because of God. I was able to work a few days a week, all while knowing Anna Benton was being cared for by her wonderful nurses and aides at the daycare. I had plenty of time off as well, for her weekly therapies and specialist appointments. Life *was* grand (and still is).

Looking back, I'm beyond grateful for the wonderful opportunity I had at the daycare. I know I was meant to be there and I'm proud to have helped start it. I also know that Justin and I are helicopter parents and there is no way we would have willingly started Anna Benton there if I had not worked there and seen first-hand, how wonderful it was—and still is. That opportunity taught me so much and helped get my foot back into the door of the working world. Her sweet nurses continue to spoil her and we all, especially "Princess AB," wouldn't have it any other way. Plus, I still get to visit with the patients when I'm there to pick her up and drop her off. Win-win!

My schedule was clearing up and I was thoroughly enjoying my new days off from work. I had finally found the work/life balance that I desperately needed. Justin and I were able to have lunch dates and Baker and I had the afternoons to do whatever we wanted.

I've got to tell you, weekdays off are amazing. They are good for the soul. I love being able to go to our favorite bakery, the movie theatre, parks, Kroger, etc. when everyone else isn't there! Small to no crowds? Yes, please!

After several changes to her medications, Anna Benton's seizures were well controlled and we were having much longer stretches between hospitalizations. We made it over an entire year without having to spend the night at what we jokingly called our second home.

Justin and I were feeling like pros at this whole parenting thing, even the special needs part of it. Life was *so* much easier. That step of faith sure turned out to have some pretty fruitful blessings, and we still had to more follow.

The following fall, Anna Benton was accepted into a preschool for children with special needs, one that she had been on the waiting list for almost three years. This precious school is a tuition free, non-profit organization which provides a Christ centered education and a supportive environment to students and their families. Because of her recent stability, we felt comfortable sending her to school, especially since it was only for half days. And even better, she continued receiving nursing care at the daycare in the afternoons, which meant twice as much therapies now too.

Everything had fallen into place beautifully. Isn't God good?

With even more exposure to special needs environments and the additional therapies, Anna Benton began to interact more with the world around her. Her reaction time from when she saw a toy to when she reached for it dropped drastically. She became much more engaged and began recognizing her name. You know it does this Mama's heart good to see her baby girl grin when she hears her named called. The staff and teachers at both the school and the daycare love her as much as we do. They have been wonderful to her and our family.

Once again, in just a matter of months, so much had changed so drastically. But this time, we were elated about it. We had taken that leap of faith, found some much needed rest, and received the Lord's abundant blessings.

> Trust in the Lord with all your heart, and do not lean on
> your own understanding. In all your ways acknowledge
> him, and he will make straight your paths.
> —Proverbs 3:5–6

12
CHAPTER

When God Speaks

God, who at various times and in various ways spoke in time
past to the fathers by the prophets, has in these last days
spoken to us by His Son, whom He has appointed heir of
all things, through whom also He made the worlds.
—Hebrews 1:1–2

In their hearts humans plan their course, but
the Lord establishes their steps.
—Proverbs 16:9

U p until this point, this book has been about the glass ceiling that
breaks every time something doesn't go according to plan. The
rest is about love. Real love. God's love. I have spoken about faith
several times. But if you're like me, you learn by examples, and I'm
more than happy to share some.

There have been many times that Justin and I stepped out in faith
and answered God's call, knowing that while we were oblivious to
what the outcome would be for taking that step, God would lead us
on the right path, and carry us through. We were blessed, and blessed

abundantly, because of being obedient to Him. I'm not saying that to brag, but I want to give credit where credit is due in order to shed light on how gracious our Lord truly is.

One of the first times I felt God speak to me was while I was in high school. I was reading my Precious Moments bible during church and a devotion from 2 Corinthians 5:15 caught my eye. It talked about once we become a Christian, we are to be changed; living for God instead of ourselves. I felt the Lord speaking to me and I underlined every word in that little devotion. Besides for obvious reasons, I knew it would be important and would come in handy eventually. And it did.

My senior year, I was asked to do the children's church sermon for a morning service, in front of the entire congregation. From the second I was asked, I knew the topic I would speak on: 2 Corinthians 5:15.

That Sunday morning, I remember asking the kids what they would think if I walked in with a purple wig, clown makeup, and crazy clothes. They all laughed, as well as the congregation, and told me I would look pretty silly. I explained that while God doesn't call us to be that extreme, He does want us to be set apart from the world; to be changed from our old ways of living and live for Him.

After I finished the message, our visiting pastor walked up to the pulpit and was very emotional with a big smile on his face. He explained that God had laid that very verse on his heart to preach that day. We were all in awe. I had never seen nor met that man before but we both showed up to church that day with the same message from the same verse. That's God!

I have mentioned several times where I felt the Lord speaking to me through a song. It's like the words jumped out at me and applied to my exact situation at that time. One song I haven't mentioned before that God laid on my heart is "I Will Rise" by Chris Tomlin. I usually keep my car radio on KLove and there are plenty of times where songs come on and I'm not really paying attention to them. I hear them; but they may not really resonate with me at that particular time. This was one of those songs.

On the morning of Anna Benton's first surgery, I literally woke up with almost every word to that song in my head, never realizing that I knew it. Honestly, I'm not so sure I did. Up until that morning, I had been somewhat of a nervous wreck. Baker had been put to sleep for ear tubes two times and he breezed through it each time. But her surgery was going to be different, long and intense; and I was a little stressed about it. Ok, a *lot* stressed...

But somehow, I woke up with a sense of peace that day and kept singing to myself, "There's a peace I've come to know, though my heart and flesh may fail. There's an anchor for my soul. I can say, 'It is well.'" How did I know those words? I had never paid attention to that song! Some people may try to discredit that somehow but I know the truth. Again, that's God!

I've also mentioned reading <u>On Milk and Honey</u> by Morgan Cheek. A friend of mine went to a women's conference where Morgan spoke and her story reminded her of mine. She said she bought a copy of her book because she felt led by the Lord to gift it to me.

Anna Benton was less than one-week post-op from having a g-tube placed and we were struggling. She was on continuous feeds at that point and I was sleeping in the bed with her to keep her from tangling her tubing. She rolls like a kamikaze when she sleeps and even with me right beside her, she managed to disconnect the feeding line from her g-tube. The pump continued to flow and because of my sleep-deprived stupor, I didn't notice. As you can imagine, we got soaked with Neutramigen and by 6:00 a.m., I was changing bedding, her clothes, and my clothes. It was a mess!

Well that same morning is when that precious book arrived in the mail. It couldn't have come at a better time. As I read Morgan's words (I read the entire book within twenty-four hours), it was if she had heard my thoughts; thoughts that I had never shared with anyone. Her story is in fact similar to mine and I felt like I had made a new friend, even though we have never met. I couldn't help but smile and say, "Was that you, God?"

One of the biggest times God showed out is with our home. We had previously listed our first home for sale when Baker was an infant. But had *zero* luck. It stayed on the market for six months and we didn't get as much as a second-look request, near less an offer. While I was disappointed, we felt it was obviously a sign that it was not time to sell it yet.

Once Anna Benton came along and I needed to stay home with her, we were so grateful for that small home and the small mortgage that came with it. Because we had not bought a larger home, we were able to afford for me to be a SAHM. Isn't God good? I may have pouted that I didn't get a larger home when I wanted it but boy, am I glad I didn't! He saw the bigger picture when I didn't.

Speaking of being a SAHM, I had been feeling a tug on my heart during the entire time I was on maternity leave with Anna Benton. The idea of being away from her scared me and I never felt completely comfortable about leaving her. I know now that God was preparing me for the decision to quit full-time nursing.

After I went to work full time and Anna Benton and I were at the medical daycare, Justin and I felt it was time to list our home for sale again. This time felt different. It wasn't just a lack of space issue. We needed to move into a better school district, one that had an excellent special needs program. We prayed about pretty much everything throughout the search process—I'm talking down to the carpet, roof, floor plan, and neighbors.

We found one home that we both loved, so much that we signed a Contingent to Sell contract and wrote a check for earnest money. I put the cart before the horse and ordered a personalized stamp with our name and new address because I was so excited.

Within a day or so, we heard word from our realtor that another family placed a full offer on the house we had a contract on; not a Contingent to Sell offer, but a *full* offer. That meant we had to decide whether to back out or make a full offer as well. I was ready to start a bidding war but Justin told me he was having reservations about the house. He loved everything about it except the fact that we would need to do some updates and repaint almost all of the interior. He would prefer for us to find a home that was move-in ready. I didn't want to hear that but we knew we needed to take some time and pray about it.

The next morning, we felt the right choice for us was to back out of the contract. Again, I was disappointed but if history was to repeat itself, this closing door was a sign to "be still and know that [He is] God" (Psalm 46:10). The only thing I begrudgingly said to Justin was that I needed him to make sure he trashed that personalized address stamp before I laid eyes on it! I had accepted that something better was in our future and I didn't need anything to change my mind. (I suppose he threw it away when it came in the mail because I never saw it. Bless his sweet soul!)

Now, on to the good part. At this point, our house had been on the market for almost a month and we decided to look again. There was a particular neighborhood Justin was interested in but I didn't know much about it. Several people he knew lived there and it was close to some great schools. He said it would actually cut thirty minutes off our drive back home to see our family in the Delta.

The first house we looked at was in that neighborhood and we looked at several other houses in surrounding areas. We both immediately fell in love with the first house and requested a second look that same day. It had everything we were looking for and more. It was pretty much brand new and was move-in ready.

As we were doing our second walk through, I felt a tug at my heart. I knew God was telling me this house would become our new home. I've never heard His audible voice but I felt Him telling me to trust Him. Standing in the living room with me holding Anna Benton and Baker running around us, I told Justin what the Lord had laid on my heart. To my surprise, he said he felt this was the one too. Instead of just getting our feet wet by signing another Contingent to Sell contract, we jumped in head first, and made an offer on the house, trusting that God would provide and our home would sell.

Instead of being worried about the possibility of having two house notes, I had a sense of peace about it all. Within a week, we got a call from our realtor. We were actually sitting in the surgery waiting room while Baker had his third set of ear tubes placed when we got the call. Our realtor said that not only did we receive an offer on our home, it was a full listing offer. That's right, a *full* offer! Tears of joy are streaming down my face as I type this, because I remember exactly how I felt in that moment and it still feels the same, years later. I sat in that waiting room crying and praying, "Thank you, Lord. Thank you."

I know all of that happened the way it did, and the order it did, because of God. We just had to trust Him and take that leap of faith. He blessed us abundantly and I am beyond grateful. Even though He doesn't have to, He proves Himself time and time again that His plan is greater than our own. Have mercy, God is good! Can I get an "Amen!"?

13

CHAPTER

Peace

I have told you these things, so that in me you may have peace. In this world you will have trouble. But take heart! I have overcome the world.
—John 16:33

I have lived through heartache, despair, and turmoil. We all have. But because of that, I can say that nothing can compare to the peace I've felt that has come from God. Philippians 4:7 says, "and the peace of God which transcends all understanding, will guard your hearts and your minds in Christ Jesus."

While my children had surgeries, the Lord gifted me peace. I never felt like I was going to come unglued if I didn't hear frequent updates from the operating room nurse. I may have cried as I handed them to the nurse anesthetist every single time but I was not fearful. Emotional? Yes. Fearful or anxious? No. That may not make sense, but that's how I felt. I was calm—no chest pains, no anxiety, just peace.

I also had a surreal sense of calm about having a second WES for Anna Benton, even with the possibility of receiving an astronomical bill. While Justin and I had prayed about it and got a game plan together for covering costs, we had no idea the surprise that was in store for us. It's so good that I having been waiting to share it with you for this very moment.

Shortly after the WES results came in and Anna Benton's diagnosis was finally discovered, a bill from the hospital came in the mail not long after. Justin and I waited to open it together and reminded each other of the budget cuts we had made to hold up our end of the bargain. Well guess what! We opened that envelope together, standing side-by-side in our kitchen, to find a "balance due" of FOUR DOLLARS.

Not $5,000.

Four dollars.

At first, we thought it was a fluke but the explanation of benefits (EOB) from our insurance company confirmed that in fact, the testing was covered! I stood in our kitchen and wept because I knew who was responsible for such an amazing blessing. It was *all* God and we praised Him for it. He gave me such peace about it all because He knew the whole time that we weren't going to have to cover the cost.

You better believe that I shouted those praises to everyone who had an ear to hear. Let me tell you, there was a celebration at the Coleman house! Justin said he was going to mail a check for double because he was so proud. I know that may have only come out to eight dollars, but that's my Justin.

Baker, Anna Benton and I love an impromptu dance party, complete with Baker's light up speakers and glow-in-the-dark beach balls. You best believe we had ourselves a shindig that night, and even Justin joined in.

God is good all the time. And all the time, God is good!

Another time that God showed out is when I eventually realized management wasn't for me anymore. I couldn't handle the stress and anxiety that came along with it. I had prayed, lost sleep, fought with myself and talked with Justin, trying to figure out the right thing to do for our family. I ultimately didn't care what stepping down may look like. I needed less stress and I needed it right then. I may have tearfully turned in my notice but I stepped out in faith, trusting that God would open the right door for me. Within a week of my resignation, I had two job offers—one I didn't even interview for.

I knew God would take care of us. I had peace that He would provide because I was following His lead. And provide, He did.

I don't want to paint a picture that I am at peace all of the time now. Justin and I both teeter-totter between phases of being completely unraveled and phases of peace. I much prefer those phases of peace but know that both bring opportunities for growth.

Like Shauna Niequist said in her book <u>Present Over Perfect</u>:

What I ache for these days is space, silence, stillness, Sabbath. I want to clear away space and noise and things to do and things to manage. I want less of everything. Less stuff. Less rushing. Less proving and pushing. Less hustle. Less snapping at my kid[] so that [he]'ll get [himself] into the car faster so we can go buy more stuff that we're going to throw away. Less consumption. Less feeling like my mind is fragmented and my stomach is bloated and my life is out of control.

I crave peace. I *need* peace.

I also know that I'm currently in a transition phase. I know what I'm doing now is not what I will be able to do forever. Eventually, I will have to work less once Anna Benton starts first grade, due to time constraints. I'm not sure what that will entail but I know that God has something big in store for our family—something that is even better suited for us. I have been telling Justin this for months. I guess you could consider this another time the Lord is speaking to me. Only time will tell what that turns out to be, but again, I'm not anxious about it. Not to sound too cheesy but like Aaron Cole and Toby Mac sing, "Don't worry at all. His love is always right on time." He always provides and His plan is greater than any I could construct on my own.

After reading several books, I kept feeling a calling to write my own. I had pretty much been blogging on social media, just without the official title. I bought <u>Present over Perfect</u> shortly after finishing <u>On Milk and Honey</u> and that's when I knew this is what I'm supposed to do.

Within minutes of reading them, I began jotting down an outline and chapter titles of what would become my own book. I wrote them on an old calendar that was crumpled in my purse, right there in the OT waiting room. Within an hour, I had filled that calendar from front-to-back. I sent a message to Justin: "I swear I'm starting to feel a calling to write a book. This may be hard. Ugly even. But this feels right. And real. This is terrifying but I swear this is the 'next thing' I've been telling you about. Does that sound weird?" His response: "Doesn't sound weird at all." Justin is a man of few words and for him, that response was practically a novel. And that was the green light I needed at the time, to take my next leap of faith. I bought a laptop on the way home and the words started flying on the pages. This book has practically written itself!

I love bragging on God. It has been cathartic to share our story and is an even greater reminder of His grace, love, and mercy. If another soul never reads it, I will be at peace because I trust in whatever the Lord has planned. It has taken me a long time to get to this place of solace but I know it is all because of Him that I am able to say it at all.

One of my favorite verses is one of the most memorized verses in the Bible (besides John 3:16). It's Philippians 4:13 but more importantly for me, verse twelve, as well as thirteen. It says, "I know what it is to be in need, and I know what it is to have plenty. I have learned the secret of being content in any and every situation, whether well fed or hungry, whether living in plenty or in want. I can do all things through Christ, who gives me strength."

I have peace knowing whatever my situation, I can handle it because my source of strength comes from the Lord. And that feeling, my friends, is priceless!

Peace I leave with you; my peace I give you. I do
not give to you as the world gives. Do not let your
hearts be troubled and do not be afraid.
—John 14:27

14

CHAPTER

A New Perspective

But seek first his kingdom and his righteousness, and all these things
will be given to you as well. Therefore, do not worry about tomorrow, for
tomorrow will worry about itself. Each day has enough trouble of its own.
—Matthew 6:33–34

Be joyful in hope, patient in affliction, faithful in prayer.
—Romans 12:12

Being a part of the world of parenting, especially special needs
parenting, has been one of my greatest honors. It has also
completely changed my perspective on pretty much everything! I
have learned to celebrate my children for who they are and how
wonderful they are. I love them for nothing more than just being
themselves.

I'm embarrassed to say this but I used to grieve myself over the
children I expected to get instead of being grateful for the ones God
gave me. (Lord, forgive me.) I mean, how ridiculous is that? My
kids may not be what the world considers mainstream, but so what?

They're amazing! And to be honest, we're all a little different in our own way! If everyone was the same, life would be pretty boring.

If there's anything my life *isn't*, it's boring. Every day typically has some sort of surprise in store for me. Because of that, it's easy to keep a sense of humor. I mean, I have to, to keep from going crazy. It's all about perspective and remembering to allow yourself some grace.

When I've kept a positive perspective and remembered to look at the bigger picture, it is easy to see God's handiwork in almost everything. I'm talking about every open and closed door, every opportunity and every hardship. Like I said before, I'm a firm believer in saying "everything happens for a reason." I feel strongly that God allowed me to become a pediatric emergency nurse, so I would know how to take care of Anna Benton. I also believe He allowed me to go through a lot of hardship as a child, in order to prepare me for adulthood.

Who knows if I would have been able to handle everything that had been thrown my way, had I not been made tough from the start? Looking back, I'm not sure if I would change anything that has happened in my life. I may not have had a picture-perfect childhood but who knows? If I had, would I have been strong enough to endure the trials of my adulthood? (At least that's the way I like to look at it. And I'm not sure you could convince me otherwise.)

A colicky infant could make a grown man cry. Having a child with a vast number of diagnoses and developmental delays brought me to my knees on more occasions than I can count. "What doesn't kill us makes us stronger." Right? I learned from my experiences and we grew closer to God with each trial.

1 Peter 1:13 says, "Therefore, prepare your minds for action, keep sober in spirit, fix your hope completely on the grace to be brought to you." I need to write this compelling verse on every mirror in my home. Honestly, I may need to tattoo it on my forehead as a reminder on the hard days, to keep my eyes fixed on the Lord and not my circumstances. He has blessed me beyond measure and the number of every good day far surpasses the number of bad days I've had. In fact, most days, "my cup runneth over" (Psalm 23:5).

My point is, we all go through trials—it's how you handle them that counts. When I pouted and wallowed in self-pity, I didn't do anyone any good- especially myself. But when I grew up, learned to lean on God and look for the positives, found a way to have a laugh, allowed myself some grace, and learned to love more fiercely, my life was changed. My perspective changed. My "Why's?" became "Why not's?" And instead of keeping my hand out, constantly *expecting* help, I learned to keep my hand out, instead to *offer* help.

I've been given multiple opportunities to share my story and witness to others, teaching of God's love and grace. I've seen the despair in parent's eyes, as they are dealing with their child's new diagnosis. I've held their hands as they are struggling to face their new realities. I share my experiences: how it felt like my world was crashing down on me when we were blindsided the day Anna Benton was born, the heaviness that I felt in my chest as I watched her go through so much, yet the endless love of God we've felt through it all.

I read Emily Perl Kingley's description of what it's like raising a child with special needs and was profoundly moved. She compares it to planning a trip to Italy, only to find your plane landing in Holland instead. Though unexpected, there is beauty to be found in "Holland," just like there's beauty to be found in the world of parenting a child with special needs. I love sharing Emily's words with other parents in hopes of comforting them and offering them an opportunity to find joy along their journey. They may not understand it at the time, but they will eventually.

I am grateful for every parent I've met who has been on a similar journey, and the peace they brought to me through their story. It is a blessing to share mine and bestow some of that peace to other families in return.

15
CHAPTER

Joy in the Journey

Though you have not seen Him, you love Him; and even though
you do not see Him now, you believe in Him and are filled
with an inexpressible and glorious joy, for you are receiving
the end result of your faith, the salvation of your souls.
—1 Peter 1:8–9

If I have learned anything over the course of my life, it is to look
for the positives in situations. Good is always there but it may be
easier to see some times, versus others. I wouldn't necessarily classify
myself as an optimist but more as a realist with a need for sanity.
Previous situations taught me that if I let fear, doubt, and bitterness
creep into my heart, I would let them live there, rent free. I would
even feed them and parade them around as if they were sitting in a
rocking chair on my front porch. Remember my friend's quote about
falling in the water and drowning?

I once heard a pastor say, "In order to live a happy life, you must
live a grateful one." An attitude of gratitude will bring happiness to
your life as well as others'. Because of so many lessons learned, it is

important for me to keep a positive outlook and remain grateful for the journey God has chosen for me. What good does it do me to live life with the glass half empty? It's much more fulfilling to live with a glass half full approach.

I will never forget our first New Year's Eve spent in our new home. We've never really been ones to partake in NYE festivities and that year was no different. I usually *try* to stay up late enough to watch the ball drop but most times, I'm asleep before Ryan Seacrest starts the countdown. That particular night, all four of us, along with our pups, were piled up on our couch watching the television. I remember looking over at them and feeling my heart start to swell. We had been blessed with a pretty uneventful winter—no hospitalizations, no surprises with croup, no curveballs thrown our way. For the most part, that winter had been pretty dull, even boring. And in that moment, I had never felt more grateful for *boring* in my life. I sat there, snuggled up with the ones I love most, looked up, and thanked God. I tightly closed my eyes and soaked up every bit of that goodness from God.

I also couldn't help but get tickled that I was thankful for boring. Who does that? I'm telling you, being the parent of a child with special needs will do that to you. We love a reason to be proud!

I know I have talked a lot about celebrating little victories, but there are so many reasons why we do that. When Anna Benton lost the milestone of saying "Mama" and "Dada," I was crushed. We have a video of her saying "Dada" but not of "Mama" because I never thought I wouldn't hear it again. Because of that, I record just about everything she does now because I don't want to miss a thing. I love replaying those videos and remembering how I felt at that time. It hurts that she doesn't speak anymore but sometimes, the hardest lessons reap the greatest rewards. I now have hours of entertainment on my phone, of my happy baby girl being her silly, giggly self.

One particular victory that I'm especially proud to share is regarding Anna Benton's g-tube. With the exception of a handful of times, for her entire life, we had never slept past 8:00 a.m., because her seizure medications are due twice a day. She gets them first thing in the morning and at night, before bedtime. We have such a routine down that we rarely have to set alarms anymore.

When waking her up for morning meds and breakfast, we inevitably ended up waking Baker as well. This has gone on, like I said, for years and Sister usually isn't thrilled about being woken up every morning. I mean, we *all* love our sleep, right?

Well, let me tell you… As much as it hurt our feelings that we couldn't make her eat enough to prevent getting a gtube, I sure appreciate that fabulous thing! Now that she has one, only one of us gets up early, gives her medicines through it, then goes back to sleep. She gets to sleep through it also and we don't wake the whole house in the process. It's amazing! Sleep is amazing! And her gtube is amazing! When she wakes up on her own, she has already been medicated and she's usually happy as a clam to be fed her breakfast. That's a little victory that we feel is a *huge* blessing and is definitely something to feel joyful about!

Speaking of blessings, I often find myself savoring little moments with my children. One of my favorites with Baker is when we were on a beach vacation and he asked me repeatedly, "Mama, is this my life?" "How long are we staying in my life?" "When are we going back to my life?" Justin and I were puzzled by Baker's "life" questions and he would get frustrated at our confusion. It took over a day of us asking what he meant before Justin realized he was calling our hotel room his life. (Isn't that precious? So oblivious, yet absolutely sweet and innocent.) We spent the rest of our week laughing about Baker's "life" and because of those precious moments, we may call a hotel room a "life," from now on. I smile every time I think about it and I hope to remember his cute little mix of words regarding *his* life for the rest of *mine*.

While on that same "life" beach vacation, Anna Benton found the ocean hilarious. As each wave rolled onto the shore, she got tickled as if it were the first time she had seen one. She let out the sweetest, biggest, belly laugh with every wave and I felt my heart swell while watching her. There I was, on the beach with my hubby and my babies, taking in all of God's goodness again.

What did I do to deserve a love like that? I have been given a multitude of opportunities for joy and I am so grateful for my blessings. Anna Benton makes the world brighter because she emits pure joy. She's dripping with it! You can't help but feel it when she's around. I may be biased but she has the best giggle in the whole world. It is not only infectious but addictive, and we find ourselves acting like fools, doing anything we can to make her laugh. Even on a day when she's not feeling like herself, you're guaranteed at least a few giggles. We may have to break out the Velcro to hear it but she laughs, nonetheless.

And my Baker man, he is a scrumptious little thing who gives the best hugs. He is so thoughtful and makes me feel loved every single day. There is something about a baby boy's love for his Mama. It's immeasurable but I can assure you, I love him even more. And that's nothing compared to how much God loves us.

Another tremendous blessing in my life is Justin. I have loved watching him change from my boyfriend, to my husband, and now our children's father. Seeing him with the kids and the love they have for each other melts my heart, making me love him even more. And let's talk about his resiliency through all of this. He went from never having held a baby or changed a diaper before Baker was born, to becoming dad extraordinaire and an honorary nurse. He can prime a g-tube pump like a boss and can mix Anna Benton's medicines with his eyes closed. (Luckily, he doesn't because things might get interesting if he did.) He's learned and grown so much over the last few years and I couldn't be prouder of him.

As Christians, we have so much to be joyful about. God is always with us and He loves us more than we could ever imagine. As John 3:16 says, "For God so loved the world, that He gave His only begotten Son, that whosoever believes in Him, will have everlasting life." I mean, as a Christian, I "love my neighbor" and all, but I can't imagine giving up Baker for them! I certainly can't fathom watching him suffer at the cost of saving someone else. It's inconceivable. While it's completely human of me to think that way, it just shows how incredible God's love is. He sacrificed His *only* Son for us in order for us to spend eternity with Him. In Him, we have the blessed assurance that He is coming back one day to take us to our eternal home in heaven (John 14:2–4). While we may have no idea what the earthly journey He has chosen for us will look like, at least we know the ending is a happy one!

I'm sure there are more challenges that lie ahead. While the thought of that possibility is kind of terrifying, we are to "stand firm in the faith; be courageous; [and] be strong" (1 Corinthians 16:13). God is *with* us and *will be* with us through it all (Joshua 1:9). He will never leave us nor forsake us. (Deuteronomy 31:6). Some trials may be even harder than what we've already faced but regardless of our circumstances, if He will bring us *to* it, He will bring us *through* it.

God has done some mighty things in my life and I take joy in that (Psalm 126:3). He has been so good to me. While it is easy to brag on Him and how He has blessed me beyond all measure, I don't want you to think that I say, "God is good," just because of those blessings. Even if He takes it all away, "He is still good" (Daniel 3:18). As a type this, Anna Benton is experiencing a monster of a stomach bug. Justin and I have been practically baptized in her body fluids, up to our elbows in Lysol, dirty diapers, and vomit. But you know what? My steel magnolia is giggling through it, He is still good, and her g-tube is what is saving us from yet another hospitalization.

So yeah, I have faced difficulties and I have been given plenty of opportunities to give up and be bitter. But like I said, I've been given a multitude of blessings that far surpass any trial He has put in my path. It is all His design. "We are afflicted in every way, but not crushed; perplexed, but not driven to despair; persecuted, but not forsaken; struck down, but not destroyed; always carrying in the body the death of Jesus, so that the life of Jesus may also be manifested in our bodies" (2 Corinthians 4:8–10). Life can be hard but we have hope. That hope is *in* and *because* of Jesus. I can say, "it is well with my soul," "because He lives," and because "she laughs."